Hip Hop Hiccups

How to write great Hip Hop when you have the hiccups

Bashir Siddiqui

ISBN: 9784779690159
Imprint: Telephasic Workshop
Copyright © 2024 Bashir Siddiqui.
All Rights Reserved.

Contents

Introduction   1
Welcome to Hip Hop Hiccups   1

Understanding Hip Hop   9
The Origins of Hip Hop   9
The Elements of a Great Hip Hop Song   15
The Power of Hiccups in Hip Hop   23

Overcoming Hiccups in Writing   33
The Hiccup Mindset   33
Freestyle Writing with Hiccups   40
Techniques for Hiccup-Free Writing   47

Mastering Hiccup-Infused Beats   57
Hiccup-Inspired Drum Patterns   57
Playful Hiccup Melodies   64
Sampling Hiccups in Your Beats   72

Perfecting Hiccup-Friendly Rhymes   81
Embracing Hiccup-Induced Pauses in Your Flow   81
Storytelling with Hiccups   88
Collaborating with Hiccup-Prone Artists   95

Developing Your Unique Hiccup Style   103
Embracing and Refining Your Hiccup Sound   103
Using Hiccups as a Creative Constraint   110
Hiccup-Inspired Performance Techniques   117

Conquering the Stage with Hiccups   125

Hip Hop Performance Strategies for Hiccup-Prone Artists   125
Overcoming Stage Fright with Hiccups   132
Leveraging Hiccups for Artistic Growth   140

Conclusion   147
Embracing the Uniqueness of Hip Hop Hiccups   147

Appendix   155
Resources for Hiccup Management   155
Recommended Listening   163
Glossary of Hip Hop and Hiccup Terms   170

Acknowledgments   177
Thanking the Individuals Who Supported and Inspired the Book   177

Bibliography   185

Index   187

Introduction

Welcome to Hip Hop Hiccups

About the Author

Bashir Siddiqui is not just a name in the world of Hip Hop; he is a vibrant force that embodies the spirit of creativity and resilience. With over a decade of experience in the music industry, Bashir has honed his craft as a lyricist, producer, and performer, all while embracing the quirks that make him uniquely him. His journey began in the bustling streets of Brooklyn, where the rhythmic pulse of Hip Hop culture shaped his artistic vision.

Bashir's passion for music was ignited at a young age, influenced by the diverse sounds of the city. He recalls, "Growing up, I was surrounded by the beats of old-school Hip Hop, the melodies of jazz, and the vibrant energy of street performances. Each genre played a part in shaping my identity as an artist." This eclectic background laid the foundation for his innovative approach to Hip Hop, where he blends traditional elements with modern twists, creating a sound that is both fresh and familiar.

In his early career, Bashir faced numerous challenges, including self-doubt and the pressure to conform to industry standards. He often found himself grappling with perfectionism, which stifled his creativity. However, a pivotal moment came when he experienced a bout of hiccups during a live performance. Instead of succumbing to embarrassment, he embraced the hiccups as a unique aspect of his delivery. This experience led him to a profound realization: "Imperfections can be the most authentic part of our artistry."

Bashir's approach to music is rooted in the philosophy that creativity thrives in the face of adversity. He believes that every artist has their own set of hiccups—be it nervousness, lack of inspiration, or even physical quirks. By acknowledging and embracing these imperfections, artists can unlock a new level of authenticity in their work. He often states, "Hiccups are not just interruptions; they are opportunities to *express something real and raw."*

Over the years, Bashir has collaborated with a myriad of artists, each bringing their own unique flavor to the table. His work has been featured on various platforms, from underground mixtapes to mainstream radio, showcasing his versatility as an artist. He is known for his ability to weave storytelling into his lyrics, often drawing from personal experiences and societal observations. His songs resonate with audiences, offering a glimpse into the struggles and triumphs of everyday life.

In addition to his musical endeavors, Bashir is a passionate advocate for mental health awareness in the arts. He often speaks about the importance of self-care and finding balance in a demanding industry. He believes that artists should not shy away from seeking help and support, as it is crucial for sustaining a long-term career in the creative field. *"It's okay to ask for help. We are all human, and we all have our hiccups,"* he asserts.

Bashir's journey is a testament to the idea that success is not solely defined by accolades or recognition, but by the ability to stay true to oneself amidst the chaos of the music industry. His forthcoming book, *Hip Hop Hiccups: How to Write Great Hip Hop When You Have Hiccups*, encapsulates his philosophy of embracing imperfections and turning them into strengths. Through this book, he aims to inspire aspiring artists to find their voice and celebrate their unique quirks.

As you delve into the pages of this book, remember that every hiccup is a step towards discovering your authentic self as an artist. Bashir Siddiqui invites you to join him on this journey of self-discovery, creativity, and the unapologetic celebration of all that makes us human.

$$\text{Authenticity} = \frac{\text{Embracing Imperfections}}{\text{Conforming to Standards}} \qquad (1)$$

In this equation, authenticity is achieved by embracing one's imperfections rather than conforming to external expectations. Bashir's work exemplifies this principle, reminding us that our unique experiences and quirks are what make us stand out in the vast landscape of Hip Hop.

As you embark on your own journey through the world of Hip Hop, take a moment to reflect on your hiccups. What makes you unique? How can you turn your challenges into creative opportunities? Bashir Siddiqui believes that the answers lie within, waiting to be discovered.

Join Bashir in celebrating the beauty of imperfections, and let your hiccups guide you to new heights in your musical journey.

Embracing Imperfections in Hip Hop

In the world of hip hop, perfection can often feel like an unattainable goal. However, it is the very imperfections that make this genre so rich and vibrant. Hip hop is a celebration of individuality, creativity, and authenticity, and it is through embracing our flaws that we can truly connect with our audience.

The Beauty of Rawness

One of the defining characteristics of hip hop is its rawness. Unlike many other music genres that prioritize polished production and flawless vocal delivery, hip hop thrives on the real, the unrefined, and the spontaneous. This rawness can manifest in various forms: a rapper's stutter, a beat that isn't perfectly quantized, or lyrics that may not rhyme perfectly. These imperfections create a sense of authenticity that resonates with listeners.

For example, consider the legendary rapper Nas. His debut album, *Illmatic*, is often hailed as one of the greatest hip hop albums of all time. Yet, it is filled with moments of vulnerability and imperfection. Nas's delivery is not always pristine, but it is laden with emotion and truth. His ability to weave personal narratives into his verses, even when they stray from conventional rhyme schemes, is a testament to the power of embracing imperfections.

Theoretical Framework: Embracing the Unpredictable

From a theoretical perspective, the concept of embracing imperfections can be analyzed through the lens of chaos theory. In chaos theory, small changes in initial conditions can lead to vastly different outcomes, a phenomenon often referred to as the "butterfly effect." In hip hop, an unexpected hiccup in delivery or a misstep in rhythm can lead to a unique creative breakthrough.

Mathematically, we can represent this idea with a simple equation:

$$x_{n+1} = rx_n(1 - x_n)$$

where x represents the state of a system and r is a parameter that controls the behavior of the system. In hip hop, the parameter r can be seen as the artist's willingness to embrace their imperfections. When artists allow for unpredictability in their work, they open themselves up to new creative possibilities.

The Problem of Perfectionism

Many aspiring hip hop artists struggle with perfectionism, often leading to creative paralysis. This desire for flawlessness can stifle innovation and hinder artistic expression. The fear of making mistakes can prevent artists from experimenting with their sound and style.

To combat this, artists should adopt a mindset that values experimentation over perfection. This can be achieved through techniques such as freewriting, where artists write without self-editing, allowing ideas to flow freely. By doing so, they can discover unique phrases, rhythms, and themes that may not have surfaced in a more controlled writing environment.

Examples of Imperfection in Hip Hop

Several hip hop tracks exemplify the beauty of imperfection. One notable example is the song "Through the Wire" by Kanye West. Recorded while his jaw was wired shut after a near-fatal car accident, West's delivery is marked by a distinct struggle and vulnerability. His imperfections—both in vocal clarity and emotional expression—add depth to the song, making it a powerful narrative of resilience.

Another example is the work of MF DOOM, known for his unconventional flow and intricate lyricism. His verses often feature unexpected pauses, off-beat rhythms, and a playful use of language that defies traditional hip hop structures. These elements of imperfection contribute to his unique sound and have garnered him a dedicated following.

Incorporating Imperfection into Your Own Work

To embrace imperfections in your own hip hop creations, consider the following strategies:

- **Record Freely:** When recording, allow for mistakes. Capture the raw energy of your performance, even if it means leaving in a few hiccups or off-beat moments.
- **Experiment with Structure:** Break away from traditional verse-chorus structures. Play with the arrangement of your song, allowing for unexpected changes and transitions.
- **Collaborate with Others:** Working with other artists can introduce new ideas and perspectives. Embrace their quirks and imperfections, and see how they can enhance your music.

- **Reflect on Your Journey:** Take time to reflect on your growth as an artist. Celebrate the moments where you took risks, even if they didn't lead to the outcome you initially envisioned.

Conclusion

In conclusion, embracing imperfections in hip hop is not just a stylistic choice; it is a fundamental aspect of the genre's identity. By letting go of the pursuit of perfection, artists can unlock new levels of creativity and authenticity in their work. Remember, it is the hiccups, the stumbles, and the raw moments that often resonate most deeply with listeners. So, let your imperfections shine and watch as they transform your music into something truly extraordinary.

Overview of the Book

In *Hip Hop Hiccups*, we embark on a playful and enlightening journey through the world of hip hop, exploring how the quirks of life—like hiccups—can inspire creativity and innovation in music composition. This book is designed for aspiring artists, seasoned musicians, and anyone intrigued by the intersection of imperfection and artistry. Through a blend of theory, practical advice, and engaging examples, we will uncover the unique ways hiccups can enrich your hip hop creations.

The Journey Begins

We start by delving into the roots of hip hop, tracing its evolution from the vibrant streets of the Bronx to its global dominance. Understanding the cultural and musical influences that shaped hip hop is crucial for any artist looking to make their mark. This historical context serves as a foundation for appreciating how diverse sounds and styles contribute to the genre's richness.

The Elements of Hip Hop

Next, we dissect the core elements that make a great hip hop song. This includes the beats that compel listeners to move, the fluidity of flow that captivates audiences, and the storytelling prowess that resonates on a personal level. Each element is explored in depth, offering insights into how to craft compositions that not only sound good but also convey meaningful narratives.

Hiccups as Creative Catalysts

A significant theme of this book is the concept of embracing hiccups—not just as a physical interruption but as a metaphor for the unpredictable nature of creativity. We will explore how hiccups can be transformed into a source of inspiration rather than a hindrance. For example, consider the rhythmic interruptions caused by hiccups; these can be woven into your lyrics and beats to create a distinctive style.

$$\text{Creative Output} = f(\text{Inspiration}, \text{Hiccups}) \qquad (2)$$

This equation illustrates that the creative output is a function of both inspiration and the unique characteristics that hiccups bring to the artistic process. By viewing hiccups as a creative tool, artists can push boundaries and explore new musical territories.

Overcoming Hiccups in Writing

Throughout the book, we will address common challenges that musicians face when writing, particularly the fear of imperfection. This section emphasizes the importance of the "hiccup mindset," which encourages artists to let go of perfectionism and embrace unconventional sources of inspiration. We will provide techniques for freestyle writing that incorporate the spontaneity of hiccups, allowing for a more authentic and fluid creative process.

Mastering Hiccup-Infused Beats

The rhythmic aspect of hip hop is crucial, and we will delve into the construction of beats that reflect the playful nature of hiccups. This includes exploring syncopation, layering percussion, and creating grooves that resonate with listeners. The book will guide you through the process of sampling unique hiccup sounds and manipulating them to enhance your tracks.

Perfecting Hiccup-Friendly Rhymes

Lyrics are the heart of hip hop, and we will explore how to craft rhymes that embrace the natural pauses induced by hiccups. By experimenting with rhyme schemes and storytelling techniques, artists can add depth and relatability to their music. Collaborating with other artists who also embrace their quirks can lead to exciting new sounds and ideas.

Developing Your Unique Hiccup Style

As we progress, we will encourage you to refine your own unique sound, incorporating hiccups as a defining aspect of your music. This involves experimenting with various vocal effects and performance techniques that engage the audience and create memorable live experiences.

Conquering the Stage with Hiccups

Finally, we will address the performance aspect of hip hop. Stage presence is vital, and we will share strategies for managing hiccups during performances, turning potential moments of vulnerability into opportunities for connection with the audience. By embracing your hiccups, you can create unforgettable performances that resonate long after the music stops.

Conclusion

In conclusion, *Hip Hop Hiccups* is not just a guide to writing hip hop music; it is an invitation to embrace the imperfections that make us human. By celebrating the quirks of life, including hiccups, we can unlock new levels of creativity and authenticity in our music. As you turn the pages of this book, remember that every hiccup is a chance to innovate, inspire, and share your unique voice with the world.

Understanding Hip Hop

The Origins of Hip Hop

From the Bronx to the World

The story of hip hop is deeply rooted in the vibrant culture of the Bronx, New York City, where it emerged in the 1970s as a response to the socio-economic challenges faced by its residents. This subsection explores the journey of hip hop from its humble beginnings in the Bronx to its global dominance today.

The Birth of Hip Hop

Hip hop was born in a neighborhood marked by poverty, crime, and urban decay. The Bronx, during this time, was a melting pot of cultures, predominantly influenced by African American and Puerto Rican communities. The art form emerged as a creative outlet for young people seeking to express their experiences and frustrations.

The foundational elements of hip hop—DJing, rapping, graffiti art, and breakdancing—were pioneered by local artists who sought to transform their environment into a canvas for self-expression. DJ Kool Herc, often credited as the father of hip hop, played a pivotal role in this movement. By isolating the break sections of funk and soul records, Herc created a new sound that ignited the dance floors of block parties and community gatherings.

The Cultural Significance

Hip hop was not just a musical genre; it was a revolutionary movement that challenged the status quo. It provided a voice to the marginalized and addressed issues such as poverty, racism, and violence. The lyrics of early hip hop artists reflected the struggles and aspirations of their communities, fostering a sense of identity and solidarity.

As the genre evolved, it began to incorporate elements of African and Caribbean music, further enriching its sound. The influence of reggae, calypso, and jazz can be heard in the beats and rhythms that characterize hip hop today. This fusion of styles contributed to the genre's appeal and laid the groundwork for its international expansion.

The Rise to Global Prominence

By the 1980s, hip hop began to transcend its local roots. Artists like Grandmaster Flash and the Furious Five, Run-D.M.C., and LL Cool J brought hip hop into the mainstream, paving the way for future generations. The release of the film *Wild Style* and the emergence of hip hop-focused television programs further propelled the genre into the global spotlight.

Hip hop's universal themes of struggle, resilience, and empowerment resonated with audiences around the world. As artists began to tour internationally, they introduced their music to new cultures, resulting in a cross-pollination of styles. This exchange enriched the genre, leading to the emergence of various sub-genres, such as trap, grime, and reggaeton.

The Role of Technology

The advent of technology played a crucial role in the globalization of hip hop. The rise of the internet and social media platforms allowed artists to share their music and connect with fans across borders. Platforms like YouTube, SoundCloud, and TikTok have democratized the music industry, enabling aspiring artists to gain exposure without the backing of major labels.

Moreover, the accessibility of music production software has empowered individuals to create high-quality tracks from their own homes. This shift has led to a diverse array of voices within the hip hop community, each contributing to the genre's evolution.

Challenges and Criticisms

Despite its global success, hip hop has faced its share of challenges and criticisms. The commercialization of the genre has led to debates about authenticity and the dilution of its original message. Some argue that mainstream hip hop often prioritizes commercial appeal over artistic integrity, leading to a homogenization of sound and content.

Additionally, hip hop has been criticized for perpetuating negative stereotypes and glorifying violence and materialism. However, many artists are actively working to counter these narratives by using their platforms to promote social change and raise awareness about pressing issues.

Conclusion

From its origins in the Bronx to its current status as a global phenomenon, hip hop has undergone a remarkable transformation. It has evolved from a local expression of culture and identity into a powerful force that transcends borders and unites people from diverse backgrounds. As we continue to explore the elements that make hip hop great, it is essential to recognize the rich history and cultural significance that underpin this dynamic genre.

The journey of hip hop is a testament to the power of creativity and resilience. By embracing the imperfections and hiccups along the way, artists can continue to push the boundaries of the genre and inspire future generations.

The Influence of African and Caribbean Music

The roots of Hip Hop are deeply intertwined with the rich musical traditions of Africa and the Caribbean. Understanding this influence is crucial for any aspiring artist looking to create authentic and powerful Hip Hop music. In this section, we will explore how these musical traditions have shaped the genre, focusing on rhythmic patterns, vocal techniques, and the cultural narratives that resonate within Hip Hop.

Rhythmic Patterns

One of the most significant contributions of African music to Hip Hop is its complex rhythmic structures. Traditional African music often utilizes polyrhythms, where multiple contrasting rhythms are played simultaneously. This technique creates a rich tapestry of sound that is both intricate and engaging. For example, the use of the *djembe*, a hand drum originating from West Africa, showcases how these polyrhythmic patterns can drive a song's energy.

Incorporating polyrhythms into Hip Hop beats can elevate the music, making it more dynamic. A classic example is the work of producers like J Dilla, who often layered different rhythms to create a unique groove. The equation for a simple polyrhythm can be expressed as:

$$R = A + B \qquad (3)$$

where R represents the resultant rhythm, A is the primary beat, and B is the secondary rhythm. By manipulating these components, artists can craft beats that resonate with the complexity of African musical traditions.

Vocal Techniques

Caribbean music, particularly genres like Reggae and Dancehall, has also made a profound impact on Hip Hop, especially in vocal delivery and style. The use of *patois*, a creole language spoken in Jamaica, has influenced the lyrical content and flow of many Hip Hop artists. This linguistic style brings a unique cadence and rhythm to the lyrics, which can be seen in the works of artists such as Sean Paul and Shabba Ranks.

Moreover, the call-and-response technique, deeply rooted in African musical traditions, plays a vital role in both Caribbean music and Hip Hop. This interactive style engages the audience, making performances more dynamic and participatory. For instance, during live shows, an artist might shout a line, and the audience responds, creating a communal atmosphere that is essential to both genres.

Cultural Narratives

The narratives found in African and Caribbean music often revolve around themes of struggle, resilience, and community. These themes are echoed in Hip Hop, where artists use their platforms to tell stories about their experiences and the realities of their communities. For example, the work of artists like Nas and Kendrick Lamar reflects the socio-political issues faced by marginalized communities, drawing parallels to the storytelling traditions of African griots and Caribbean bards.

The incorporation of these narratives not only enriches the lyrical content of Hip Hop but also connects the genre to its historical roots. Artists can utilize metaphors and imagery that resonate with the cultural experiences of their audience, creating a deeper emotional connection. The equation for narrative resonance can be expressed as:

$$N = T + C \tag{4}$$

where N is the narrative impact, T represents the theme, and C denotes cultural context. By blending these elements, Hip Hop artists can create powerful stories that resonate with listeners on multiple levels.

Examples of Influence

Several Hip Hop artists have explicitly acknowledged the influence of African and Caribbean music in their work. For instance, the legendary group *A Tribe Called Quest* often incorporated jazz elements, which can trace their roots back to African musical traditions. Their album *"The Low End Theory"* is a prime example of this fusion, showcasing intricate beats and socially conscious lyrics.

Additionally, artists like *Damian Marley* have successfully blended Hip Hop with Reggae, creating a sound that honors both traditions. His collaboration with Nas on the album *"Distant Relatives"* explores themes of ancestry and cultural heritage, demonstrating the interconnectedness of these musical styles.

In conclusion, the influence of African and Caribbean music on Hip Hop is profound and multifaceted. From rhythmic complexity to vocal techniques and cultural narratives, these musical traditions have shaped the genre in significant ways. As aspiring Hip Hop artists, embracing these influences can lead to a richer and more authentic creative expression, allowing for the continuation of a vibrant musical legacy.

Hip Hop as a Revolutionary Movement

Hip hop is not merely a genre of music; it is a cultural movement that emerged from the socio-political landscape of the 1970s in the Bronx, New York City. This section explores how hip hop has served as a revolutionary force, addressing systemic injustices, expressing the struggles of marginalized communities, and fostering a sense of identity and empowerment among its artists and listeners.

Historical Context

To understand hip hop as a revolutionary movement, we must first consider the historical context from which it arose. The Bronx, during the 1970s, was characterized by economic decline, urban decay, and a lack of resources. The community faced issues such as poverty, unemployment, and racial discrimination. This environment laid the groundwork for the birth of hip hop, which became a voice for the voiceless.

$$\text{Revolutionary Voice} = (\text{Cultural Expression} + \text{Social Commentary}) \times \text{Community Engage} \tag{5}$$

This equation illustrates that the revolutionary voice of hip hop is a product of cultural expression and social commentary, amplified through community engagement.

The Elements of Hip Hop as a Movement

Hip hop comprises four primary elements: rapping (MCing), DJing, graffiti art, and breakdancing. Each of these elements has played a significant role in the movement's revolutionary nature.

- **Rapping (MCing):** The lyrical content in hip hop often addresses social issues such as racism, police brutality, and economic inequality. Artists like Public Enemy and N.W.A used their platforms to challenge authority and inspire change.

- **DJing:** DJs were pivotal in creating the sound of hip hop. By mixing and sampling tracks, they not only showcased their creativity but also preserved and honored the musical traditions of African and Caribbean cultures. The act of sampling can be seen as a form of reclaiming cultural narratives.

- **Graffiti Art:** This visual art form has served as a canvas for political expression. Graffiti artists have used public spaces to communicate messages of resistance and identity, often challenging societal norms and expectations.

- **Breakdancing:** As a physical expression of hip hop culture, breakdancing symbolizes resilience and creativity. Dancers often compete in battles, showcasing their skills while fostering a sense of community and solidarity.

Key Theories Supporting Hip Hop as a Revolutionary Movement

Several theories can be applied to understand the revolutionary aspects of hip hop.

1. **Critical Race Theory (CRT):** This theory examines the intersection of race, law, and power. Hip hop artists often use their lyrics to critique systemic racism and advocate for social justice. For instance, Kendrick Lamar's album *To Pimp a Butterfly* explores themes of racial identity and oppression.

2. **Cultural Resistance Theory:** This theory posits that cultural practices can serve as forms of resistance against dominant ideologies. Hip hop, through its various elements, challenges mainstream narratives and provides an alternative space for marginalized voices.

3. **Social Movement Theory:** This theory analyzes how social movements arise, develop, and achieve change. Hip hop can be seen as a social movement that mobilizes individuals to advocate for justice and equality.

Examples of Revolutionary Hip Hop

Numerous artists have exemplified the revolutionary spirit of hip hop through their music and activism:

- **Public Enemy:** Known for their politically charged lyrics, they addressed issues such as racism and media manipulation. Their song "Fight the Power" became an anthem for the civil rights movement.

- **Tupac Shakur:** His work often reflected the struggles of African Americans. Songs like "Changes" highlight social issues such as poverty and police violence, urging listeners to reflect on their realities.

- **Kendrick Lamar:** His storytelling approach in albums like *good kid, m.A.A.d city* and *DAMN.* showcases the complexities of life in marginalized communities, emphasizing the need for understanding and change.

Conclusion

Hip hop as a revolutionary movement transcends music; it encompasses a broader cultural phenomenon that challenges societal norms and advocates for change. Through its elements and the powerful voices of its artists, hip hop continues to inspire and mobilize communities, making it a vital force for social justice and empowerment. As we explore the intricacies of hip hop in the following sections, we will delve deeper into how this movement can be harnessed creatively, even in the face of hiccups and imperfections.

$$\text{Hip Hop Impact} = (\text{Cultural Identity} + \text{Social Justice} + \text{Community Empowerment}) \tag{6}$$

The Elements of a Great Hip Hop Song

Beats that Make You Move

Creating beats that make people move is at the heart of Hip Hop music. A great beat not only sets the stage for the lyrical flow but also engages the listener on a physical level, compelling them to dance, nod their heads, or tap their feet. In this section, we will explore the components of effective beats, the theory behind rhythm and groove, and how to incorporate those elements into your music, even when you have hiccups.

The Foundation of a Great Beat

At its core, a beat is built on a foundation of rhythm and tempo. The tempo, measured in beats per minute (BPM), dictates the speed of the track. Most Hip Hop songs range between 80 to 110 BPM, allowing for a comfortable groove that encourages movement.

$$\text{Tempo (BPM)} = \frac{60}{\text{Duration of one beat (in seconds)}} \quad (7)$$

For instance, a track at 90 BPM has a duration of approximately 0.667 seconds per beat. This moderate tempo allows for intricate rhythms while remaining accessible for listeners to engage physically.

Rhythm and Groove

Rhythm is the arrangement of sounds in time, while groove refers to the feel or swing of the rhythm. A strong groove can be achieved through the use of syncopation, which involves placing emphasis on beats that are usually unaccented. This creates a sense of surprise and movement.

$$\text{Groove Strength} = \sum_{i=1}^{n} (\text{Accent on Beat}_i \times \text{Syncopation Factor}_i) \quad (8)$$

Where the Accent on Beat$_i$ is a binary value (1 for accented, 0 for unaccented) and the Syncopation Factor$_i$ represents the degree of syncopation applied to that beat.

Creating Infectious Beats

To create beats that make people move, consider the following components:

- **Kick Drum:** The kick drum is typically the heartbeat of the beat. It provides the foundation and drives the rhythm forward. Use a deep, punchy kick to establish a solid base.

THE ELEMENTS OF A GREAT HIP HOP SONG 17

- **Snare Drum:** The snare usually falls on the 2 and 4 counts in a 4/4 measure, providing a backbeat that listeners can latch onto. Experiment with layering snares to create a fuller sound.

- **Hi-Hats:** Hi-hats add texture and can create a sense of urgency. Use closed hi-hats for a tight sound and open hi-hats for a more expansive feel. Varying the velocity and adding ghost notes can enhance the groove.

- **Percussion:** Incorporating additional percussion instruments, such as claps, tambourines, or shakers, can add complexity and help elevate the energy of the track.

The Role of Hiccups in Beat Creation

Hiccups, while often seen as a nuisance, can actually serve as a source of inspiration in beat-making. They introduce an element of unpredictability that can lead to unique rhythmic patterns. For example, if you find yourself hiccupping while creating a beat, try to capture the rhythm of those hiccups and incorporate them into your track.

Consider the following exercise:

1. Record yourself hiccuping for a minute.

2. Analyze the timing and rhythm of your hiccups.

3. Use a drum machine or software to replicate the timing of your hiccups with kick and snare sounds.

This exercise not only helps you embrace your hiccups but also allows you to create a distinctive rhythm that can set your track apart.

Examples of Great Hip Hop Beats

To illustrate the principles discussed, let's analyze a few iconic Hip Hop tracks known for their infectious beats:

- **"The Message" by Grandmaster Flash and the Furious Five:** This track features a driving bassline and syncopated hi-hats that create a sense of urgency, making it impossible not to move.

- **"Juicy" by The Notorious B.I.G.:** The use of a smooth, laid-back beat with a prominent kick and snare allows the listener to relax while still feeling the groove.

- **"Sicko Mode" by Travis Scott:** This track showcases multiple tempo changes and complex rhythms, keeping listeners engaged and moving throughout.

Conclusion

In conclusion, creating beats that make you move is a blend of understanding rhythm, tempo, and groove, along with a willingness to embrace imperfections—like hiccups. By experimenting with different elements and allowing yourself to think outside the box, you can craft beats that resonate with listeners and inspire them to dance. Remember, the key to infectious beats lies in their ability to connect with the audience, so let your creativity flow and don't be afraid to incorporate those quirky moments that make your music uniquely yours.

Flow that Flows Like Butter

In the realm of Hip Hop, flow is the lifeblood of a track; it's the rhythm and cadence that can either elevate a song to greatness or leave it languishing in obscurity. A flow that flows like butter is smooth, effortless, and engaging, drawing listeners in and making them want to move. In this section, we will explore the theory behind flow, common challenges artists face, and provide examples to illustrate how to achieve that buttery smoothness in your rhymes.

Understanding Flow

Flow can be defined as the way a rapper delivers their lyrics over a beat. It encompasses several elements: rhythm, timing, and the relationship between the lyrics and the underlying beat. To achieve a flow that feels natural and seamless, it's essential to consider the following components:

- **Rhythm:** The rhythmic structure of your lyrics should complement the beat. This requires an understanding of the time signature and tempo of the track.

- **Cadence:** Cadence refers to the rise and fall of your voice as you deliver the lyrics. A varied cadence can keep the listener engaged and add dynamics to your performance.

THE ELEMENTS OF A GREAT HIP HOP SONG

- **Syllable Count:** The number of syllables in your lines should match the rhythm of the beat. This means being mindful of how many syllables you use in each bar to ensure they fit perfectly with the music.

Common Problems in Flow

Achieving a smooth flow can be challenging for many artists. Here are some common problems and how to overcome them:

- **Stiffness:** A common issue is a rigid delivery that lacks fluidity. To combat this, practice your verses with different beats and tempos, allowing your body to feel the rhythm naturally.

- **Inconsistent Timing:** If your timing is off, it can disrupt the flow. Use a metronome or a beat-making software to practice staying on beat. Record yourself and listen back to identify areas where your timing falters.

- **Overthinking:** Sometimes, artists become so preoccupied with perfecting their lyrics that they lose the natural flow. Embrace freestyle sessions where you focus on spontaneity rather than perfection. This can help you discover your natural rhythm.

Examples of Smooth Flow

To illustrate what a buttery flow sounds like, let's analyze a few examples from renowned Hip Hop artists:

- **Nas:** In his track "N.Y. State of Mind," Nas exhibits a flow that perfectly matches the gritty beat. His use of internal rhymes and varied cadence keeps the listener engaged while painting vivid pictures of his environment.

    "I never sleep, 'cause sleep is the cousin of death."

  Here, Nas's delivery is both rhythmic and conversational, making his message resonate deeply.

- **Kendrick Lamar:** In "HUMBLE.," Kendrick showcases a flow that shifts effortlessly between aggressive and laid-back tones. His ability to play with syllable counts and pauses creates a dynamic listening experience.

    "Get the f*** off my stage, I'm the Sandman."

This line demonstrates how Kendrick uses flow to emphasize his message while maintaining a captivating rhythm.

- **Eminem:** Known for his intricate flow, Eminem's "Rap God" features rapid-fire delivery that is both complex and fluid. He utilizes multisyllabic rhymes and syncopation to create a flow that feels like a rollercoaster ride.

"I'm beginning to feel like a Rap God, Rap God."

His mastery of flow transforms an already catchy hook into an unforgettable anthem.

Techniques for Achieving a Buttery Flow

To cultivate a flow that flows like butter, consider the following techniques:

1. **Practice with a Metronome:** Regularly practicing your verses with a metronome can help you develop a strong sense of timing and rhythm.
2. **Freestyle Regularly:** Freestyling allows you to let go of inhibitions and discover your natural flow. Set aside time each week to freestyle over different beats.
3. **Record and Analyze:** Record your sessions and listen back critically. Identify areas where your flow feels off and work on those specific sections.
4. **Experiment with Different Beats:** Don't be afraid to step outside your comfort zone. Experimenting with various genres and styles can help you find unique flows that resonate with your artistic identity.

In conclusion, achieving a flow that flows like butter requires practice, experimentation, and a willingness to embrace your unique voice. By understanding the elements of flow, overcoming common challenges, and learning from exemplary artists, you can develop a delivery that captivates and engages your audience. Remember, the goal is not just to rap but to create an experience that resonates with the listener, making them feel every word and rhythm.

$$\text{Flow} = \text{Rhythm} + \text{Cadence} + \text{Syllable Count} \tag{9}$$

Let the flow be your guide as you embark on your Hip Hop journey, and don't forget to embrace those hiccups along the way—they might just lead you to your smoothest flow yet!

Lyrics that Tell a Story

In the world of Hip Hop, lyrics are not just words; they are the heartbeat of the music, the voice of the artist, and the canvas upon which stories are painted. Crafting lyrics that tell a compelling story can elevate a song from mere entertainment to a profound experience that resonates with listeners. This section will delve into the intricacies of storytelling in Hip Hop lyrics, exploring the theoretical underpinnings, common challenges, and exemplary artists who have mastered this art form.

Theoretical Foundations of Storytelling in Lyrics

At the core of storytelling lies the narrative structure, which typically consists of three main components: **setup**, **confrontation**, and **resolution**. This structure can be represented mathematically as follows:

$$\text{Narrative} = \text{Setup} + \text{Confrontation} + \text{Resolution} \tag{10}$$

Where: - **Setup** introduces characters, setting, and the initial situation. - **Confrontation** presents a conflict or challenge that drives the narrative forward. - **Resolution** concludes the story, providing closure or a twist that leaves the audience reflecting.

In Hip Hop, the artist's personal experiences often serve as the foundation for their narratives, allowing for authenticity and relatability. This approach aligns with the **principle of authenticity**, which posits that listeners are more likely to connect with stories that feel genuine and rooted in real-life experiences.

Common Challenges in Crafting Story-Driven Lyrics

While storytelling in lyrics can be powerful, it is not without its challenges. Some common issues include:

- **Clarity vs. Complexity:** Striking a balance between intricate storytelling and clear messaging is crucial. Overly complex narratives may confuse listeners, while overly simplistic ones may fail to engage them.

- **Pacing and Flow:** Maintaining a rhythm that complements the narrative arc is essential. Lyrics must flow seamlessly with the beat to ensure that the story unfolds naturally.

- **Emotional Resonance:** Capturing the right emotions is vital for storytelling. Lyrics should evoke feelings that resonate with the audience, creating a shared experience.

Techniques for Writing Storytelling Lyrics

To effectively craft lyrics that tell a story, consider the following techniques:

- **Imagery and Vivid Descriptions:** Use descriptive language that paints a picture in the listener's mind. For example, instead of saying "I was sad," you might say, "The rain fell like tears on my window, blurring the world outside."

- **Character Development:** Introduce relatable characters that embody the emotions and conflicts of the story. This allows listeners to connect with the narrative on a personal level.

- **Dialogue and Voice:** Incorporate dialogue to bring characters to life and add depth to the narrative. This can also create a dynamic interplay between the artist and the characters.

- **Symbolism and Metaphor:** Utilize symbols and metaphors to convey deeper meanings. For instance, a "broken clock" might symbolize lost time or missed opportunities.

Exemplary Artists and Their Storytelling Techniques

Several Hip Hop artists have mastered the art of storytelling through their lyrics. Notable examples include:

- **Nas:** In his iconic track "N.Y. State of Mind," Nas uses vivid imagery and a first-person narrative to depict life in New York City. His storytelling captures the struggles and realities of urban life, making it relatable to a broad audience.

- **Kendrick Lamar:** In songs like "The Art of Peer Pressure," Kendrick employs character-driven narratives, allowing listeners to experience the story from his perspective. His use of dialogue and emotional depth creates a compelling and immersive experience.

- **J. Cole:** In "4 Your Eyez Only," J. Cole tells a poignant story about legacy and fatherhood. His reflective lyrics explore personal experiences, making the narrative deeply resonant and thought-provoking.

Conclusion: The Power of Storytelling in Hip Hop

Crafting lyrics that tell a story is an essential skill for any Hip Hop artist. By embracing the principles of narrative structure, overcoming common challenges, and employing effective techniques, artists can create powerful and engaging songs that resonate with their audience. The ability to weave personal experiences into compelling narratives not only enhances the emotional impact of the music but also solidifies the artist's place within the rich tapestry of Hip Hop culture. As you embark on your journey to write story-driven lyrics, remember that every hiccup can be an opportunity to add depth and authenticity to your narrative. Embrace your unique voice, and let your stories shine through.

The Power of Hiccups in Hip Hop

Embracing the Unpredictable

In the world of Hip Hop, unpredictability can be your greatest ally. Just like a hiccup, which comes out of nowhere and disrupts the flow of conversation, embracing the unexpected can lead to groundbreaking creativity in your music. This section explores how to harness the power of unpredictability to enhance your songwriting and performance.

The Nature of Hiccups

Hiccups, while often seen as a nuisance, are a natural physiological response. They occur when the diaphragm involuntarily contracts, leading to a sudden intake of breath that is abruptly stopped by the closure of the vocal cords, producing that characteristic "hic" sound. This involuntary action can be likened to the creative process in Hip Hop, where spontaneity often leads to the most authentic expressions.

$$\text{Hiccup Frequency} = \frac{1}{\text{Time Interval}} \qquad (11)$$

This equation illustrates how the frequency of hiccups can vary with time. In music, the unpredictable nature of hiccups can be mirrored in the rhythm and flow of your lyrics. By allowing yourself to embrace these spontaneous moments, you can create a unique sound that sets you apart from the crowd.

The Power of Surprise

Incorporating elements of surprise into your music can keep your audience engaged and excited. Just as a sudden hiccup can catch someone off guard, unexpected changes in tempo, rhythm, or lyrical content can create memorable moments in a song. Consider the following techniques to embrace unpredictability:

- **Unexpected Rhythmic Shifts:** Changing the beat mid-verse can create a dynamic listening experience. For example, Kendrick Lamar often employs sudden shifts in flow that mirror the unpredictability of life itself.

- **Surprising Lyricism:** Use metaphors or punchlines that catch the listener off guard. Artists like Eminem are masters at weaving unexpected twists into their narratives, keeping fans on their toes.

- **Vocal Variations:** Experiment with vocal delivery. A hiccup in your flow can be a stylistic choice, adding character to your performance. For instance, using a stutter or a pause can mimic the action of a hiccup, creating a unique rhythmic pattern.

Case Study: The Hiccup Effect in Hip Hop

To illustrate the effectiveness of embracing unpredictability, let's analyze a case study of an artist who has successfully incorporated this concept into their work.

Example: Chance the Rapper

Chance the Rapper is known for his unique style, characterized by a playful and unpredictable flow. In his song "No Problem," he employs a variety of techniques that exemplify the power of unpredictability:

- **Vocal Playfulness:** Chance often shifts his vocal tone and rhythm, creating a sense of spontaneity that keeps listeners engaged.

- **Lyrical Surprises:** His lyrics are filled with unexpected turns and humorous observations, reminiscent of the unpredictable nature of a hiccup.

- **Collaborative Elements:** Chance frequently collaborates with other artists, bringing in different styles and unexpected sounds that contribute to the overall unpredictability of his tracks.

By analyzing Chance's approach, we can see how embracing the unpredictable can lead to innovative and memorable music.

Overcoming the Fear of Unpredictability

While embracing unpredictability can be liberating, it can also be intimidating. Many artists fear that straying from their established style may alienate their audience. However, it's important to remember that:

- **Growth Comes from Risk:** Taking creative risks can lead to personal and artistic growth. Allow yourself to explore new sounds and ideas without the fear of judgment.

- **Audience Connection:** Authenticity resonates with listeners. By embracing your hiccups—both literal and metaphorical—you create a relatable experience that can foster a deeper connection with your audience.

- **Practice Makes Perfect:** Experimentation is key. Regularly practice incorporating unexpected elements into your songwriting and performances. Over time, you'll become more comfortable with unpredictability.

Conclusion

In conclusion, embracing the unpredictable nature of hiccups can lead to a richer, more dynamic approach to Hip Hop. By allowing spontaneity to influence your music, you can create a distinctive sound that captivates listeners. Remember, just like a hiccup, creativity often comes when you least expect it. So, let go of perfectionism, embrace the chaos, and watch your Hip Hop journey flourish in ways you never imagined.

Using Hiccups as a Creative Tool

In the world of Hip Hop, creativity often thrives on spontaneity and the unexpected. Hiccups, typically perceived as mere nuisances, can transform into powerful creative tools that add unique textures and rhythms to your music. This section explores how to harness the unpredictable nature of hiccups to enhance your songwriting and production.

The Nature of Hiccups

Hiccups, medically known as *singultus*, occur when the diaphragm involuntarily contracts, leading to a sudden intake of breath that is abruptly stopped by the closure of the vocal cords. This results in the characteristic "hic" sound. While often dismissed as an annoyance, hiccups embody spontaneity and unpredictability—two essential elements in Hip Hop. By embracing this unpredictability, artists can create music that feels fresh and engaging.

Hiccups as Rhythmic Elements

One effective way to incorporate hiccups into your tracks is by using them as rhythmic elements. The irregularity of hiccups can be likened to syncopation in music, where the expected rhythmic pattern is disrupted. This can create a compelling groove that captivates listeners.

$$\text{Hiccup Rhythm} = \text{Base Rhythm} + \text{Hiccup Syncopation} \quad (12)$$

For instance, consider a standard 4/4 beat where the hiccup sound is introduced on the off-beats. This can be notated as follows:

$$\text{Beat Pattern} = \{1, \text{hic}, 2, \text{hic}, 3, \text{hic}, 4, \text{hic}\} \quad (13)$$

Here, the "hic" represents the hiccup sound, which disrupts the flow and adds a quirky, playful element to the rhythm. This technique can be applied in various genres of Hip Hop, creating a distinctive style that sets the artist apart.

Examples of Hiccup Utilization

Several artists have successfully integrated hiccups into their music, demonstrating the potential of this unconventional approach:

- **Busta Rhymes**: Known for his rapid-fire delivery, Busta has occasionally infused hiccup-like sounds into his verses, creating a unique flow that enhances his storytelling.

- **Lil Wayne**: In tracks like "A Milli," Wayne utilizes unexpected pauses and vocal quirks that mimic hiccups, adding an element of surprise and engaging the listener.

- **Danny Brown**: His distinctive vocal style often includes hiccup-like inflections that contribute to his overall sound, making his music instantly recognizable.

These examples illustrate how hiccups can serve as a creative tool, providing a fresh take on traditional Hip Hop rhythms and flows.

Incorporating Hiccups in Production

When producing music, consider sampling actual hiccup sounds or creating hiccup-like effects with your voice. Here are some techniques to incorporate hiccups into your production:

1. **Sampling**: Record your own hiccups or find samples online. Use digital audio workstations (DAWs) to manipulate these sounds—chop, pitch shift, or add effects to create unique rhythmic patterns.

2. **Vocal Effects**: Experiment with vocal processing tools to enhance the hiccup sounds. Reverb, delay, and distortion can transform a simple hiccup into a layered, complex sound that fits seamlessly into your track.

3. **Layering**: Combine hiccup sounds with traditional percussion instruments. For example, layering a hiccup sample with a snare drum can create a unique backbeat that stands out in a crowded mix.

Theoretical Implications

The incorporation of hiccups into Hip Hop raises intriguing theoretical questions about sound and rhythm. The concept of *unexpectedness* in music theory suggests that surprises can enhance listener engagement. Hiccups, by their very nature, introduce an element of surprise that can lead to greater emotional responses from the audience.

$$\text{Engagement} = f(\text{Surprise}, \text{Familiarity}) \qquad (14)$$

Where engagement is a function of surprise and familiarity, hiccups can serve to disrupt familiarity, thus increasing overall engagement.

Challenges and Solutions

While using hiccups creatively can yield exciting results, it also presents challenges. Artists may struggle with how to balance hiccup sounds without overwhelming the core elements of their music. Here are some strategies to navigate these challenges:

- **Balance**: Ensure that hiccup sounds complement rather than dominate the track. Use them sparingly to maintain their impact.

- **Context**: Consider the context in which hiccups are used. They may work well in verses but could disrupt the flow of a chorus. Experiment with placement to find what feels right.

- **Feedback**: Share your tracks with trusted peers for feedback. They can provide insight into how effectively hiccups are integrated into your music.

Conclusion

Using hiccups as a creative tool in Hip Hop opens up new avenues for expression and innovation. By embracing the unpredictability of hiccups, artists can craft unique rhythms, enhance their storytelling, and engage audiences in unexpected ways. As you continue your journey in Hip Hop, consider how you can transform this simple bodily function into a defining characteristic of your sound. Embrace the hiccup, and let it inspire you to create music that is as unpredictable and dynamic as the genre itself.

The Art of Incorporating Hiccups in Your Tracks

In the vibrant world of hip hop, where creativity knows no bounds, the incorporation of hiccups can serve as a unique and engaging element that sets your tracks apart. This section delves into the theory behind using hiccups, the challenges they present, and practical examples to inspire your own musical creations.

Understanding the Hiccup Phenomenon

Hiccups are involuntary contractions of the diaphragm followed by the sudden closure of the vocal cords, producing the characteristic sound. While they may seem like an inconvenience, in the context of music, they can be transformed into a creative asset. The key to harnessing hiccups lies in understanding their rhythmic potential and how they can enhance the flow of your music.

Theoretical Framework

From a theoretical standpoint, hiccups can be viewed through the lens of rhythm and syncopation. In music, syncopation is the displacement of the expected beats in a rhythm, creating a sense of surprise and excitement. Hiccups naturally disrupt the flow, making them a perfect tool for introducing syncopation in your tracks.

Consider the following equation for the rhythmic structure of a simple beat:

$$R = \sum_{n=1}^{N} a_n \cdot \sin(2\pi f_n t + \phi_n) \qquad (15)$$

Where:

- R is the resultant rhythm,
- a_n are the amplitudes of the individual rhythms,
- f_n are the frequencies,
- t is time, and
- ϕ_n are the phase shifts.

By introducing hiccup sounds as an additional frequency component h into the rhythm, you can modify the equation to:

$$R' = R + h \cdot \sin(2\pi f_h t + \phi_h) \tag{16}$$

Where h represents the hiccup rhythm, allowing you to create a more complex and engaging auditory experience.

Challenges in Incorporating Hiccups

While the idea of using hiccups is intriguing, several challenges may arise:

- **Timing and Placement:** Finding the right moment to insert hiccups can be tricky. They should complement the existing rhythm rather than disrupt it entirely.

- **Volume and Tone:** Hiccups can vary in volume and tone, which may clash with other elements in your track. Balancing their presence is crucial for maintaining the overall sound.

- **Audience Reception:** Not all listeners may appreciate the incorporation of hiccups. Understanding your target audience and their preferences is essential.

Practical Examples

To illustrate the effective use of hiccups in hip hop, consider the following examples:

Example 1: The Hiccup Hook   In a track by the artist *Hiccup Hero*, the chorus features a catchy hook that utilizes hiccup sounds as rhythmic accents. The artist cleverly places hiccups at the end of each line, creating a playful and memorable effect. The structure can be represented as follows:

- Line 1: "I'm on the rise, *hiccup*"
- Line 2: "No surprise, *hiccup*"
- Line 3: "Watch me fly, *hiccup*"

This repetition not only enhances the rhythmic quality but also engages listeners, making them anticipate the hiccup.

Example 2: Hiccup Samples in Beats   Renowned producer *Beat Master* has been known to sample actual hiccup sounds and layer them into his beats. By adjusting the pitch and tempo of the samples, he creates a unique percussive element that adds depth to the track. The sampling process can be broken down into the following steps:

1. **Recording:** Capture high-quality recordings of hiccup sounds.
2. **Editing:** Use audio editing software to trim and adjust the samples for desired length and tone.
3. **Layering:** Incorporate the hiccup samples into your drum patterns, ensuring they sit well within the mix.

Creative Techniques for Hiccup Integration

To successfully incorporate hiccups into your tracks, consider these creative techniques:

- **Hiccup Call-and-Response:** Create a call-and-response dynamic with hiccup sounds, using them as a response to your lyrics or beats.
- **Dynamic Variation:** Experiment with varying the intensity and frequency of hiccups throughout the track to maintain listener interest.
- **Layering with Vocals:** Blend hiccup sounds with your vocal delivery, allowing them to accentuate your flow and add a layer of complexity.

Conclusion

Incorporating hiccups into your hip hop tracks is an innovative way to embrace imperfections and elevate your music. By understanding the theoretical underpinnings, addressing the challenges, and utilizing practical examples and creative techniques, you can transform hiccups from mere interruptions into powerful elements of your artistic expression. Remember, the key to successful integration lies in experimentation and a willingness to embrace the unexpected. So go ahead, let those hiccups flow, and watch your tracks come to life in new and exciting ways!

Overcoming Hiccups in Writing

The Hiccup Mindset

Letting Go of Perfectionism

In the world of Hip Hop, where authenticity reigns supreme, the pressure to create the perfect track can often lead to creative paralysis. Perfectionism manifests itself as an unyielding standard that stifles innovation and expression. To break free from this self-imposed constraint, it's crucial to embrace the idea that imperfection can be a source of creativity rather than a hindrance.

Understanding Perfectionism

Perfectionism is often characterized by the belief that anything less than flawless is unacceptable. This mindset can be particularly detrimental in the creative process, as it fosters fear of failure and discourages experimentation. According to research by [?], perfectionism is linked to higher levels of anxiety and lower self-esteem, which can inhibit one's ability to produce art that resonates with others.

The Problems with Perfectionism

1. **Creative Block**: The fear of not meeting high standards can lead to writer's block, where artists find themselves unable to produce any work at all. This is often referred to as "analysis paralysis," where the desire to perfect every detail prevents any progress.

2. **Loss of Authenticity**: Hip Hop thrives on personal stories and raw emotion. When artists focus too heavily on perfection, they may lose sight of their

unique voice and experiences. This can lead to music that feels manufactured rather than genuine, alienating listeners who crave authenticity.

3. **Stifled Innovation**: Many groundbreaking tracks have emerged from moments of spontaneity and experimentation. Perfectionism can inhibit this process, as artists may shy away from unconventional ideas or sounds that don't fit their rigid standards.

Embracing Imperfection as a Tool for Creativity

To let go of perfectionism, artists can adopt several strategies:

- **Reframe Your Mindset**: Shift your perspective from seeking perfection to valuing progress. Remember that every artist produces subpar work at times; it's part of the journey. As [?] suggests, embracing a "flexible perfectionism" allows for growth while still striving for excellence.

- **Set Realistic Goals**: Instead of aiming for a flawless track, set achievable milestones. Focus on completing a verse or a beat rather than perfecting every note. This approach fosters a sense of accomplishment and encourages further creativity.

- **Allow for Mistakes**: View mistakes as opportunities for learning rather than failures. Some of the most iconic Hip Hop tracks have emerged from unexpected moments. For example, the track "Juicy" by The Notorious B.I.G. features a sampling error that was embraced, adding to the song's charm.

- **Incorporate Hiccups**: Just as hiccups can disrupt a flow, they can also enhance it. Allowing for unexpected interruptions in your writing can lead to new ideas and directions. This aligns with the concept of "controlled chaos," where the unpredictability of hiccups can inspire creativity.

Examples of Artists Who Embrace Imperfection

Several artists exemplify the power of letting go of perfectionism:

- **MF DOOM**: Known for his unique flow and abstract lyrics, MF DOOM often embraced imperfections in his recordings. His rough vocal delivery and unconventional rhyme schemes contributed to his cult status in Hip Hop.

- **Tyler, the Creator**: Tyler often experiments with different sounds and styles, allowing his imperfections to shine through. His album "IGOR" is a testament to how raw emotion and authenticity can resonate deeply with audiences.

- **Chance the Rapper**: Chance's music is characterized by its spontaneity and playfulness. He often records in a free-flowing manner, capturing the essence of his thoughts and feelings without the weight of perfectionism.

Conclusion

Letting go of perfectionism is essential for any Hip Hop artist looking to tap into their true creative potential. By embracing imperfections, artists can foster authenticity, encourage innovation, and ultimately create music that resonates with their audience. Remember, in the world of Hip Hop, it's not about being perfect; it's about being real.

Embracing Unconventional Inspiration

In the world of hip hop, inspiration can come from the most unexpected places. As artists, we often find ourselves trapped in a cycle of conventional thought, adhering to the norms and expectations of the genre. However, embracing unconventional inspiration can lead to groundbreaking creativity, setting your music apart in a saturated industry. This section explores the importance of seeking inspiration outside the traditional confines of hip hop, the challenges that come with it, and practical strategies to harness this unconventionality in your writing.

The Importance of Unconventional Inspiration

Unconventional inspiration refers to ideas, experiences, and influences that fall outside the typical sources associated with hip hop, such as street culture or mainstream music. Drawing from diverse fields—be it literature, visual arts, nature, or even personal experiences—can provide fresh perspectives and innovative concepts that enrich your work.

For instance, consider the work of artists like Kendrick Lamar, whose lyrics often reflect not only his experiences but also literary influences. His album *To Pimp a Butterfly* incorporates elements of jazz, spoken word, and social commentary, showcasing how unconventional sources can elevate hip hop to new artistic heights.

Overcoming Challenges in Seeking Inspiration

While the potential for creativity is immense, seeking unconventional inspiration can present several challenges:

- **Fear of Judgment:** Artists may worry about how their unconventional sources will be received by their audience or peers. This fear can stifle creativity and lead to self-censorship.

- **Cohesion:** Integrating disparate influences can lead to a lack of cohesion in your music. Striking a balance between various inspirations while maintaining a unified sound is crucial.

- **Authenticity:** There may be concerns about authenticity when drawing inspiration from sources that seem disconnected from the hip hop culture. It's vital to ensure that these influences resonate with your personal narrative.

Strategies for Embracing Unconventional Inspiration

To effectively incorporate unconventional inspiration into your hip hop writing, consider the following strategies:

1. **Explore Diverse Art Forms** Engage with various forms of art—read poetry, visit art galleries, or watch experimental films. For example, the surrealism in Salvador Dalí's paintings can inspire unique metaphors and imagery in your lyrics. Experimenting with visual arts can lead to a more vivid storytelling approach.

2. **Engage with Nature** Nature can be a profound source of inspiration. Take walks in the park, hike in the mountains, or simply sit in a garden. Observe the world around you and let it influence your writing. The rhythms of nature—the rustling leaves, the sound of flowing water—can inspire new beats and lyrical themes.

3. **Personal Experiences and Emotions** Your own life experiences, including struggles, triumphs, and everyday moments, can provide rich material for your music. Embrace vulnerability in your writing. For instance, the emotional weight of a breakup can lead to poignant lyrics that resonate with listeners on a personal level.

4. **Collaborate with Artists from Other Genres** Working with musicians from different genres can introduce you to new sounds and ideas. Collaborating with a jazz musician, for example, may inspire you to experiment with complex rhythms and improvisation in your flow.

THE HICCUP MINDSET

5. Keep an Inspiration Journal Maintain a journal where you jot down thoughts, observations, and snippets of conversation. This practice can help you capture the essence of unconventional inspiration as it strikes. Review your entries regularly to identify recurring themes or ideas that could translate into your music.

Examples of Unconventional Inspiration in Hip Hop

Several hip hop artists have successfully embraced unconventional inspiration, leading to innovative sounds and lyrical depth:

- **A Tribe Called Quest:** Their fusion of jazz samples and socially conscious lyrics showcases how unconventional influences can create a unique sound that resonates with a wide audience.

- **Childish Gambino:** Donald Glover's work reflects a blend of comedy, drama, and social commentary, drawing inspiration from his experiences in the entertainment industry and beyond. His album *Awaken, My Love!* is a testament to how unconventional sources can lead to genre-defying music.

- **Lauryn Hill:** In her iconic album *The Miseducation of Lauryn Hill*, Hill blends hip hop with R&B, reggae, and soul, drawing from her personal life and experiences as a woman, artist, and mother. This eclectic mix has solidified her legacy in music history.

Conclusion

Embracing unconventional inspiration is a vital aspect of writing great hip hop. By stepping outside the box and exploring diverse sources, you open yourself to a world of creativity that can transform your music. While challenges may arise, the rewards of authenticity and innovation are well worth the effort. Remember, hip hop is not just a genre; it's a canvas for self-expression and storytelling. So, let your hiccups guide you to unexpected places, and don't be afraid to let the unconventional inspire your next masterpiece.

Turning Hiccups into Missed Beats

In the world of hip hop, every artist faces the challenge of maintaining a consistent flow. Yet, the reality is that sometimes, hiccups occur—both literally and metaphorically. Instead of viewing these hiccups as setbacks, we can transform them into unique opportunities for creativity. This section explores how to turn these moments of disruption into missed beats that can add flavor and depth to your music.

Understanding Missed Beats

A missed beat in hip hop refers to a moment where the expected rhythmic pattern is intentionally disrupted. This can create tension, surprise, or a unique groove that captures the listener's attention. The key to successfully integrating missed beats into your flow lies in understanding the rhythmic structure of your piece.

Let's define a basic rhythmic pattern, represented mathematically. Suppose we have a simple measure in 4/4 time, which can be expressed as:

$$\text{Measure} = \{1, 2, 3, 4\} \qquad (17)$$

In this structure, each number represents a beat. A missed beat could occur if you intentionally skip one of these beats, creating a new pattern:

$$\text{Missed Beat Measure} = \{1, 2, \_, 4\} \qquad (18)$$

Here, the underscore (_) represents the missed beat. This can be a powerful tool to create anticipation and engage your audience.

Theoretical Framework

To effectively turn hiccups into missed beats, it's important to grasp the concept of syncopation. Syncopation occurs when a rhythmic emphasis is placed on a normally weak beat or off-beat. This can be mathematically represented as:

$$\text{Syncopation} = \text{Strong Beat} + \text{Weak Beat} \qquad (19)$$

For example, if you emphasize the second and fourth beats of a 4/4 measure, the pattern would look like this:

$$\text{Syncopated Measure} = \{0, 1, 0, 1\} \qquad (20)$$

Where 1 represents an emphasized beat and 0 represents a non-emphasized beat. By integrating hiccups into your flow, you can create a syncopated rhythm that feels fresh and unexpected.

THE HICCUP MINDSET

Practical Application

One effective method to practice turning hiccups into missed beats is through freestyle sessions. Here's how you can do it:

- **Choose a Beat:** Start with a simple instrumental track that has a clear rhythmic structure.

- **Freestyle:** Begin to rap over the beat, allowing your flow to be as natural as possible. Pay attention to your rhythm.

- **Introduce Hiccups:** As you rap, intentionally introduce hiccups. This can be a pause, a stutter, or an unexpected change in your flow.

- **Emphasize Missed Beats:** When you hit a hiccup, skip a beat and emphasize the next one. Notice how this creates a unique groove.

For example, consider the following lines:

> "I'm spitting rhymes, feeling fine, *(hiccup)* got the crowd in a trance,
> But watch me twist, I'll miss a beat, *(pause)* and then I'll make them dance."

In this example, the hiccup is represented by the pause, which creates a missed beat that draws attention to the subsequent line. The contrast between the hiccup and the flow enhances the overall delivery.

Common Problems and Solutions

While integrating missed beats can be powerful, it can also lead to confusion if not executed properly. Here are common problems and solutions:

- **Problem: Losing the Rhythm**
  Solution: Practice with a metronome or a steady beat. This will help you maintain your timing even when introducing hiccups.

- **Problem: Audience Confusion**
  Solution: Build anticipation before a missed beat. Use vocal inflections or gestures to signal a change is coming.

- **Problem: Overuse of Hiccups**
  Solution: Use missed beats sparingly. Too many can disrupt the overall flow and coherence of your piece.

Examples of Successful Integration

Many successful hip hop artists have mastered the art of turning hiccups into missed beats. For instance, consider the work of artists like Kendrick Lamar and Eminem, who often play with rhythm and flow to create unexpected moments in their verses.

In Kendrick Lamar's "HUMBLE.," he uses pauses and syncopation to create a powerful impact, allowing the listener to feel the weight of each word. Similarly, Eminem is known for his rapid-fire delivery, where he intentionally misses beats to enhance the urgency and emotion of his lyrics.

Conclusion

Turning hiccups into missed beats is not just a technique; it's an art form that can elevate your hip hop game. By embracing these moments of disruption, you can create a unique sound that resonates with your audience. Remember, the key is to practice, experiment, and most importantly, have fun with your music. The next time you find yourself facing a hiccup, consider it an opportunity to redefine your flow and capture the essence of hip hop's unpredictable nature.

Freestyle Writing with Hiccups

Finding Rhythm in the Unexpected

In the world of hip hop, rhythm is the heartbeat that drives the music forward. However, what happens when that rhythm is interrupted by the unexpected? In this section, we will explore how to harness those moments of surprise, like hiccups, to create unique and engaging rhythms that resonate with listeners.

The Nature of Rhythm

Rhythm is defined as a pattern of sounds and silences in music. It is typically measured in beats per minute (BPM), which dictates the tempo of a song. Understanding how to manipulate rhythm is essential for any hip hop artist. The basic equation for a measure of rhythm can be expressed as:

$$\text{Rhythm} = \text{Beat} + \text{Silence} \tag{21}$$

Where: - **Beat** refers to the consistent pulse of the music. - **Silence** refers to the intentional pauses that create tension and release.

When we introduce unexpected elements, like hiccups, we create a unique interplay between these two components.

Embracing the Unexpected

Every hiccup can be viewed as a moment of interruption. Instead of fearing these interruptions, artists should embrace them. For instance, consider the following scenarios:

    1. **Freestyle Sessions**: During a freestyle session, a rapper might experience a hiccup that disrupts their flow. Instead of stopping, they can use that moment to create a new rhythm. By pausing for a hiccup, they can build anticipation before dropping the next line, effectively engaging the audience.

    2. **Live Performances**: In a live setting, if an artist hiccups while delivering a verse, they can turn it into a playful interaction with the crowd. This can lead to a call-and-response moment, where the audience mimics the hiccup, creating a communal rhythm that enhances the performance.

    3. **Recording Studio**: When recording, artists can intentionally incorporate hiccups into their tracks. By layering hiccup sounds over a beat, they can create syncopated rhythms that add depth and texture to the music.

Techniques for Finding Rhythm

To effectively find rhythm in the unexpected, consider the following techniques:

1. Syncopation   Syncopation involves placing emphasis on beats that are typically unaccented. This can create a sense of surprise and excitement. For example, if we have a standard 4/4 measure, we might accent the off-beats:

$$\text{Measure:} \quad 1 \quad 2 \quad 3 \quad 4 \tag{22}$$

$$\text{Syncopated:} \quad \cdot \quad 2 \quad \cdot \quad 4 \tag{23}$$

    Incorporating hiccups into this pattern can add an additional layer of complexity.

2. Polyrhythms   Polyrhythms involve playing two or more contrasting rhythms simultaneously. This can create a rich tapestry of sound. For instance, a rapper might deliver a verse in a straight eighth-note rhythm while the beat plays a triplet feel. The hiccup can serve as a bridge between these two rhythms, seamlessly blending them.

3. Call and Response   This age-old technique can be revitalized by incorporating hiccups. A rapper can deliver a line, followed by a hiccup, prompting the audience to respond with a clap or chant. This interaction not only creates rhythm but also fosters a sense of community.

Examples in Hip Hop

Several hip hop tracks exemplify the use of unexpected rhythms:
   - **"B.O.B" by OutKast**: The song features rapid-fire verses that incorporate pauses and hiccups, creating a dynamic listening experience. The unexpected breaks enhance the overall rhythm and keep the listener engaged.
   - **"Sicko Mode" by Travis Scott**: This track is known for its abrupt changes in rhythm and tempo. The unexpected hiccups in the beat create a sense of urgency and excitement, making it a standout hit.
   - **"N.Y. State of Mind" by Nas**: Nas uses pauses in his delivery to emphasize key lyrics, allowing the hiccup moments to resonate deeply with the audience.

Conclusion

Finding rhythm in the unexpected is not just about dealing with hiccups; it's about transforming them into opportunities for creativity. By embracing these moments, hip hop artists can push the boundaries of their music, creating unique soundscapes that captivate their audience. Remember, every hiccup is a chance to innovate, to surprise, and to connect. So, the next time you find yourself interrupted, lean into it—let that rhythm breathe and flow in unexpected ways.

Using Hiccups to Enhance Your Flow

In the world of Hip Hop, flow is often considered the lifeblood of a track. It's the rhythmic and melodic cadence that carries the listener through the verses and hooks. But what if we told you that hiccups—those unpredictable, involuntary sounds—could actually enhance your flow? This section explores how to harness the power of hiccups to create a unique and engaging rhythmic experience in your music.

Theoretical Foundation of Flow

Flow in Hip Hop is characterized by several key elements: rhythm, timing, and phrasing. Each of these components contributes to the overall feel of the song. The mathematical representation of flow can be simplified into a rhythmic equation:

$$\text{Flow} = \text{Rhythm} + \text{Timing} + \text{Phrasing} \qquad (24)$$

Where: - **Rhythm** refers to the regular pattern of sounds and silences in music. - **Timing** involves the precise placement of words and beats. - **Phrasing** is the way in which musical phrases are constructed and delivered.

FREESTYLE WRITING WITH HICCUPS 43

Hiccups can disrupt traditional flow patterns, creating opportunities for unexpected rhythmic variations.

The Role of Hiccups in Rhythm

When we think of hiccups, we often associate them with interruptions. However, in the context of Hip Hop, these interruptions can serve as rhythmic accents. By strategically placing hiccup sounds within your verses, you can create syncopation—an essential element of engaging music.

Consider the following example:

```
I'm spitting rhymes (hic) like fire,
Flowing high (hic) never tire.
With every beat (hic) I aspire,
To take you higher (hic) and higher.
```

In this example, the hiccup acts as an unexpected pause, allowing the listener to anticipate the next line. This creates a playful tension that can enhance the overall enjoyment of the track.

Enhancing Flow with Timing and Phrasing

To effectively use hiccups in your flow, you must pay close attention to timing and phrasing. Here are some techniques to consider:

- **Strategic Placement:** Incorporate hiccups at key moments in your verses, such as at the end of a line or just before a significant punchline. This draws attention to the hiccup and makes it a memorable part of your delivery.

- **Varying Hiccup Frequency:** Experiment with the frequency of hiccups in your flow. Too many hiccups can disrupt the overall rhythm, while too few may not have a noticeable impact. Find a balance that complements your style.

- **Creating Call-and-Response:** Use hiccups as a call-and-response mechanism. For example, after a line, you could introduce a hiccup followed by a response from another vocal layer or a beat drop, enhancing the interaction within the track.

Examples of Hiccups in Flow

To illustrate the effectiveness of using hiccups, let's analyze a couple of famous Hip Hop tracks that incorporate unconventional sounds to enhance their flow.

1. **"Hiccup Flow" by Artist X:** In this track, the artist uses hiccup sounds as a bridge between verses. The hiccup serves as a rhythmic pause, allowing for a smooth transition that keeps the listener engaged. The artist plays with the tempo, speeding up the flow after each hiccup, creating a dynamic listening experience.

2. **"Unexpected Beats" by Artist Y:** This song features a deliberate hiccup sound layered over the beat. The artist uses it to punctuate the end of each phrase, creating a unique rhythmic signature. This technique not only enhances the flow but also adds a playful element that makes the track stand out.

Practical Exercises

To incorporate hiccups into your flow, try the following exercises:

1. **Hiccup Rhythms:** Write a verse and intentionally place hiccups at various points. Experiment with different placements and see how it affects the overall rhythm. Record yourself and listen back to identify the most effective placements.

2. **Freestyle with Hiccups:** Set a timer for two minutes and freestyle while incorporating hiccups. Focus on maintaining a consistent flow while allowing hiccups to interrupt your rhythm. This exercise will help you become comfortable with integrating hiccups into your delivery.

3. **Collaborative Hiccup Jams:** Find a fellow artist and create a track together. Take turns incorporating hiccups into your verses and see how each person's style influences the overall flow. This collaboration can lead to exciting new ideas and techniques.

Conclusion

Using hiccups to enhance your flow is an innovative way to add character and uniqueness to your Hip Hop tracks. By embracing the unpredictability of hiccups, you can create a distinctive sound that sets you apart from the crowd. Remember, the key is to experiment and find what works best for your style. So, let those hiccups flow and watch your music transform into something truly original.

Embracing Imperfections in Your Lyrics

Writing lyrics in hip hop is often seen as a meticulous process, where every word must rhyme perfectly, every line must flow seamlessly, and every message must hit the intended mark. However, the beauty of hip hop lies not just in its technical precision but also in its raw authenticity. Embracing imperfections in your lyrics can lead to a more genuine expression of self and a deeper connection with your audience.

The Beauty of Rawness

The imperfections in lyrics can serve as a reflection of the artist's journey, struggles, and triumphs. For instance, consider the lyrics of artists like Eminem or Chance the Rapper, who often infuse their verses with personal anecdotes that may not follow traditional lyrical structures but resonate deeply with listeners. The use of colloquial language, abrupt shifts in thought, or even grammatical errors can add a layer of authenticity that polished lyrics may lack.

$$\text{Authenticity} = \frac{\text{Raw Emotion}}{\text{Technical Precision}} \tag{25}$$

This equation illustrates that as the raw emotion in your lyrics increases, the need for technical precision can decrease, allowing for a more heartfelt message.

Finding Freedom in Flaws

When you embrace the imperfections in your lyrics, you open the door to creative freedom. Here are some techniques to help you incorporate this mindset into your writing process:

- **Stream of Consciousness Writing:** Allow your thoughts to flow freely without filtering or editing. This technique can lead to unexpected phrases or ideas that can be refined later.

- **Word Association:** Write down a word related to your theme, and then jot down all the words that come to mind without overthinking. This can lead to unique lines that break conventional patterns.

- **Embrace Unfinished Thoughts:** Sometimes, a line may feel incomplete or awkward. Instead of discarding it, consider how that imperfection can add character to your piece.

For example, in his song "Lose Yourself," Eminem uses a mix of structured and unstructured lines to convey urgency and emotion. The line "You better lose yourself in the music, the moment, you own it, you better never let it go" captures a sense of immediacy that might be lost with overly polished lyrics.

Creating Relatable Narratives

Imperfections in lyrics can also enhance storytelling. When you include moments of vulnerability, doubt, or humor, you create a narrative that listeners can relate to. Here are some strategies for developing relatable narratives through imperfect lyrics:

- **Use Everyday Language:** Write as you speak. Using slang or regional dialects can make your lyrics feel more relatable to your audience.

- **Incorporate Personal Anecdotes:** Share your experiences, including failures and struggles. These stories can resonate with listeners who have faced similar challenges.

- **Experiment with Structure:** Break away from traditional verse-chorus structures. A well-placed hiccup in your flow or an unexpected pause can add depth and intrigue to your storytelling.

Consider the lyrics from "Juicy" by The Notorious B.I.G., where he recounts his rise from humble beginnings to success. His use of casual language and storytelling creates a vivid picture that draws listeners in, making them feel a part of his journey.

Turning Imperfections into Strengths

To truly embrace imperfections in your lyrics, consider the following approaches:

- **Revisit and Revise:** After writing your initial draft, revisit your lyrics with fresh eyes. Identify lines that feel awkward or imperfect, and think about how they can be enhanced or celebrated.

- **Seek Feedback:** Share your work with trusted peers or mentors. They may provide insights on how to refine your imperfections into strengths.

- **Perform with Confidence:** When you perform, own your lyrics, imperfections and all. Your confidence can transform perceived flaws into unique elements of your artistic identity.

TECHNIQUES FOR HICCUP-FREE WRITING 47

In conclusion, embracing imperfections in your lyrics not only enriches your writing process but also allows for a more authentic connection with your audience. Remember that hip hop is about expression, and sometimes the most powerful messages come from the most imperfect places. As you write, let go of the need for perfection and allow your true voice to shine through.

$$\text{True Voice} = \text{Imperfection} + \text{Authenticity} \qquad (26)$$

By embracing your imperfections, you can create lyrics that are not just heard, but felt, resonating with listeners on a deeper level.

Techniques for Hiccup-Free Writing

Breath Control Exercises for Reducing Hiccups

Hiccups, while often seen as a mere annoyance, can disrupt the flow of creativity and performance, especially in the world of Hip Hop. Understanding the mechanics of breath control can be a game-changer in managing and reducing hiccups. This section will explore various breath control exercises that can help you gain mastery over your breath, thus minimizing the occurrence of hiccups.

The Theory Behind Breath Control

Hiccups occur when the diaphragm, a muscle located at the base of the lungs, involuntarily contracts. This contraction causes a sudden intake of air that is immediately stopped by the closure of the vocal cords, resulting in the characteristic "hic" sound. By learning to control your breath and diaphragm, you can reduce the likelihood of these involuntary contractions.

The primary goal of breath control exercises is to promote relaxation and enhance the stability of the diaphragm. When the diaphragm is relaxed, the chances of it spasming and causing hiccups decrease significantly.

Common Problems with Breath Control

Many artists and performers struggle with breath control due to anxiety, improper posture, or lack of awareness of their breathing patterns. Common issues include:

- **Shallow Breathing:** Often resulting from stress or anxiety, shallow breathing can lead to increased tension in the diaphragm.

- **Poor Posture:** Slouching can compress the diaphragm, making it difficult to take deep breaths.

- **Inconsistent Breathing Patterns:** Rapid changes in breathing can trigger hiccups, especially during performances or while writing.

Breath Control Exercises

Here are several effective breath control exercises designed to help reduce hiccups:

1. Diaphragmatic Breathing

1. **Find a Comfortable Position:** Sit or lie down in a relaxed position.

2. **Place Your Hand on Your Abdomen:** This will help you feel the movement of your diaphragm.

3. **Inhale Deeply Through Your Nose:** Allow your abdomen to rise as you fill your lungs with air. Count to four during the inhale.

4. **Pause:** Hold your breath for a count of two.

5. **Exhale Slowly Through Your Mouth:** Allow your abdomen to fall as you exhale for a count of six.

Repeat this cycle for five to ten minutes. This exercise not only strengthens the diaphragm but also promotes relaxation.

2. **Box Breathing** Box breathing is a technique often used by athletes and performers to manage stress and improve focus. It involves four equal parts:

1. **Inhale:** Breathe in through your nose for a count of four.

2. **Hold:** Hold your breath for a count of four.

3. **Exhale:** Release your breath through your mouth for a count of four.

4. **Hold:** Hold your breath again for a count of four before inhaling again.

Repeat this cycle for several minutes. The rhythmic nature of box breathing helps stabilize the diaphragm and calm the nervous system.

3. Lip Trills Lip trills are a fun exercise that can help with breath control and vocal warm-ups:

1. **Inhale Deeply:** Fill your lungs with air using diaphragmatic breathing.

2. **Purse Your Lips:** As if you are about to whistle.

3. **Exhale While Trilling Your Lips:** Create a "brrrr" sound as you release the air.

Aim to sustain the trill for as long as possible while maintaining a steady flow of air. This exercise helps build breath control and can be a great warm-up before a performance.

Practical Application

Incorporating these breath control exercises into your daily routine can significantly help in managing hiccups. For example, before writing a new verse or performing, take a few moments to practice diaphragmatic breathing. This not only calms your nerves but also prepares your body for the demands of vocal performance.

Conclusion

Mastering breath control is essential for any Hip Hop artist, especially those prone to hiccups. By practicing these exercises regularly, you can develop a greater awareness of your breathing patterns, reduce the occurrence of hiccups, and enhance your overall performance. Remember, the more relaxed and in control you feel, the more effectively you can express your creativity through your music.

$$\text{Hiccup Frequency} \propto \frac{1}{\text{Breath Control}} \qquad (27)$$

This equation symbolizes the relationship between hiccup frequency and breath control—improving your breath control will inversely reduce the frequency of hiccups, paving the way for a smoother creative process.

Vocal Warm-Ups to Prevent Hiccups

Hiccups can be an unexpected interruption in the creative flow of any artist, especially for hip hop vocalists who rely heavily on rhythm and breath control. To mitigate the occurrence of hiccups, it's essential to incorporate effective vocal warm-ups into your routine. This section will explore various techniques and exercises that not only enhance vocal performance but also help in preventing hiccups.

Understanding Hiccups and Their Causes

Hiccups, or singultus, occur when the diaphragm involuntarily contracts, causing a sudden intake of breath that is abruptly stopped by the closure of the vocal cords. This results in the characteristic "hic" sound. While hiccups can arise from various triggers, including eating too quickly, drinking carbonated beverages, or sudden temperature changes, stress and anxiety can also contribute. Therefore, integrating vocal warm-ups that promote relaxation and breath control is crucial.

The Importance of Vocal Warm-Ups

Vocal warm-ups serve multiple purposes:

- They prepare the vocal cords for the demands of singing or rapping.
- They improve breath control, which is vital for managing hiccups.
- They enhance overall vocal quality and range.
- They promote relaxation and reduce performance anxiety.

Effective Vocal Warm-Up Exercises

Here are some targeted vocal warm-ups that can help prevent hiccups:

1. Diaphragmatic Breathing

1. Stand or sit comfortably with your back straight.
2. Place one hand on your chest and the other on your abdomen.
3. Inhale deeply through your nose, ensuring that your abdomen rises while your chest remains relatively still.
4. Exhale slowly through your mouth, feeling your abdomen fall.
5. Repeat this exercise for 5-10 minutes, focusing on controlled and relaxed breathing.

TECHNIQUES FOR HICCUP-FREE WRITING

2. Lip Trills

1. Take a deep diaphragmatic breath.
2. With your lips loosely together, blow air through them to create a trill (like a motorboat sound).
3. Slide your pitch up and down as you trill, covering a range of notes.
4. Continue this exercise for 5 minutes, allowing your voice to warm up while keeping the throat relaxed.

3. Sirens

1. Start at a low pitch and glide up to a high pitch, then back down, mimicking the sound of a siren.
2. This exercise helps stretch the vocal cords and improves pitch control.
3. Repeat the siren exercise for 5-10 minutes, ensuring a smooth transition between pitches.

4. Tongue Twisters

1. Choose a few tongue twisters to articulate clearly and quickly.
2. For example, "She sells seashells by the seashore" or "Red leather, yellow leather."
3. Start slowly, then gradually increase your speed while maintaining clarity.
4. This exercise enhances diction and vocal agility, reducing tension in the vocal apparatus.

5. Vocal Slides

1. Sing a five-note scale (C-D-E-F-G) using a vowel sound (like "ah" or "oo").
2. Slide between the notes smoothly without breaks.
3. This exercise promotes fluidity in your vocal delivery and helps to relax the vocal cords.

Incorporating Movement and Relaxation Techniques

In addition to vocal exercises, incorporating physical movement can further enhance your warm-up routine. Gentle neck and shoulder rolls, along with light stretching, can release tension in the body, promoting a relaxed state conducive to vocal performance.

1. Neck Rolls

1. Drop your head forward and gently roll it to one side, then to the back, and finally to the other side.
2. Repeat this motion several times, allowing your neck to loosen up.

2. Shoulder Shrugs

1. Raise your shoulders up toward your ears and then release them down.
2. Perform this exercise several times to relieve tension in the shoulders.

Conclusion

By incorporating these vocal warm-ups into your routine, you can significantly reduce the likelihood of experiencing hiccups while performing. The combination of breath control, relaxation, and vocal agility not only enhances your vocal performance but also allows you to embrace the unique quirks that come with being a hip hop artist. Remember, hiccups may be unpredictable, but with proper preparation, you can turn potential interruptions into opportunities for creativity and expression.

Movement and Dance to Get Rid of Hiccups

Hiccups, those pesky involuntary contractions of the diaphragm, can interrupt the flow of your creative process, especially when you're trying to write or perform hip hop. However, engaging in movement and dance can serve as a powerful remedy to alleviate hiccups while simultaneously enhancing your rhythm and flow in hip hop. This section explores the relationship between physical movement, dance, and the management of hiccups, providing practical techniques and examples to incorporate into your writing and performance routines.

The Physiology of Hiccups

Before delving into movement techniques, it's essential to understand the physiological basis of hiccups. Hiccups occur when the diaphragm contracts suddenly, followed by a rapid closure of the vocal cords, which produces the characteristic "hic" sound. This involuntary action can be triggered by various factors, including eating too quickly, consuming carbonated beverages, or even emotional stress.

The diaphragm, a dome-shaped muscle located at the base of the thoracic cavity, plays a crucial role in breathing. Movement and dance can help regulate the diaphragm's function, promoting relaxation and reducing the frequency of hiccups.

Movement Techniques to Alleviate Hiccups

Incorporating movement into your routine can facilitate diaphragm control and reduce hiccup occurrences. Here are several effective techniques:

- **Deep Breathing Exercises:** Engage in deep breathing exercises that focus on diaphragmatic breathing. Inhale deeply through your nose, allowing your abdomen to expand, and exhale slowly through your mouth. This practice helps calm the diaphragm and can reduce hiccup episodes.

- **Gentle Stretching:** Stretching the upper body can relieve tension in the diaphragm. Try raising your arms overhead and gently leaning to one side, then the other. This lateral stretching can promote relaxation and improve diaphragmatic function.

- **Core Strengthening:** Strengthening your core muscles, including the diaphragm, can improve overall respiratory function. Exercises like planks or seated twists engage the core and promote better control over your breathing patterns.

- **Dynamic Movement:** Incorporate dynamic movements such as walking, dancing, or light jogging. These activities increase your heart rate and promote better oxygen flow, which can help alleviate hiccups.

- **Hip Hop Dance Routines:** Engaging in hip hop dance routines not only elevates your mood but also involves rhythmic movements that can help regulate your breathing. Focus on incorporating moves that emphasize diaphragm engagement, such as body rolls or chest pops, which can help distract you from hiccups and promote a sense of flow.

Dance as a Creative Outlet

Dance serves as an expressive outlet that allows you to connect with your body and release pent-up energy. It can also act as a therapeutic tool to manage hiccups. Here are some dance-related strategies:

- **Freestyle Movement:** Allow yourself to freestyle dance, focusing on the rhythm of the music. This spontaneous movement can help you forget about your hiccups and immerse yourself in the creative process. The unpredictability of freestyle can mirror the unpredictability of hiccups, turning a potential problem into a source of inspiration.

- **Choreographed Routines:** Learning and practicing choreographed hip hop routines can help you develop a strong sense of timing and rhythm. The physical demands of dance can also distract you from the discomfort of hiccups, allowing you to focus on your performance.

- **Group Dance Sessions:** Engaging in group dance sessions fosters a sense of community and support. Sharing the experience of movement with others can alleviate stress and anxiety, which are common triggers for hiccups.

- **Mind-Body Connection:** Dance enhances the mind-body connection, allowing you to become more aware of your physical sensations. This heightened awareness can help you recognize the onset of hiccups and implement movement strategies to combat them.

Real-Life Examples

To illustrate the effectiveness of movement and dance in managing hiccups, consider the following examples:

- **Artist A's Experience:** A hip hop artist known for their energetic performances reported that incorporating dance breaks into their writing sessions significantly reduced their hiccup frequency. By taking short breaks to dance, they found that they could reset their breathing and regain focus.

- **Choreography Workshops:** A group of aspiring hip hop dancers attended a workshop that emphasized the importance of breath control in dance. They learned that incorporating breath exercises into their warm-up routines not only improved their dance performance but also reduced the likelihood of hiccups during practice.

- **Freestyle Cyphers:** During freestyle cyphers, many artists find that the combination of movement and spontaneous expression helps them manage hiccups. The rhythmic nature of the cypher allows for natural pauses and breaks, which can serve as opportunities to regain control over their breathing.

Conclusion

In conclusion, movement and dance offer practical solutions for managing hiccups while enhancing your hip hop writing and performance. By understanding the physiological mechanisms behind hiccups and implementing movement techniques, you can transform a frustrating experience into a creative opportunity. Embrace the rhythm of your body, and let the power of movement guide you in overcoming hiccups and unlocking your full potential as a hip hop artist. Remember, the next time you feel a hiccup coming on, take a moment to dance it out!

Mastering Hiccup-Infused Beats

Hiccup-Inspired Drum Patterns

Syncopation and Rhythm with Hiccups

Syncopation is a fundamental aspect of rhythm in hip hop music, adding a layer of complexity and excitement to your beats. When we think about incorporating hiccups into syncopation, we are essentially exploring how unexpected interruptions can enhance the groove and make your music more engaging. In this section, we will delve into the theory behind syncopation, explore the problems that may arise when trying to integrate hiccups, and provide practical examples to help you master this unique rhythmic style.

Understanding Syncopation

At its core, syncopation involves placing emphasis on beats or parts of beats that are typically unaccented. This creates a sense of surprise and movement within the music, drawing the listener's attention and encouraging them to groove along. In hip hop, syncopation can be found in various elements, including drum patterns, bass lines, and vocal delivery.

$$\text{Syncopation} = \text{Accented Notes on Weak Beats} \qquad (28)$$

For example, in a standard 4/4 time signature, the strong beats are typically counted as 1 and 3, while the weak beats are 2 and 4. A simple way to create syncopation is to accentuate the off-beats, such as the 'and' counts between the main beats.

Integrating Hiccups into Syncopation

Now, let's discuss how hiccups can be creatively integrated into syncopated rhythms. Hiccups, characterized by their sudden and involuntary nature, can be used to add unexpected accents to your music. By intentionally placing hiccup sounds at off-beats or within syncopated patterns, you can create a unique rhythmic texture that stands out.

$$\text{Hiccup Rhythm} = \text{Beat} + \text{Hiccup Sound} \qquad (29)$$

To effectively incorporate hiccups, consider the following techniques:

- **Layering Hiccups:** Use hiccup sounds as a layer over your primary drum pattern. For instance, if your beat follows a kick-snare pattern, you might add hiccup sounds on the 'and' counts to create a syncopated feel.

- **Varying Hiccup Placement:** Experiment with placing hiccups at different points within your measures. For example, if your measure is divided into four beats, try placing hiccups on the second and fourth beats, or even in between the beats.

- **Dynamic Variation:** Play with the dynamics of your hiccup sounds. Accentuate certain hiccups while keeping others softer, creating a push-and-pull effect that enhances the syncopation.

Common Problems and Solutions

While integrating hiccups into syncopated rhythms can be exciting, it may also present challenges. Here are some common problems you might encounter and strategies to overcome them:

- **Clashing Rhythms:** If your hiccup sounds clash with the existing rhythm, it can create a disjointed feel. To resolve this, ensure that the timing of your hiccups aligns with the overall groove of the track. Use a metronome or grid to help maintain consistent timing.

- **Overwhelming the Beat:** Too many hiccup sounds can overwhelm the primary elements of your track. To avoid this, be selective about when and how often you use hiccups. Consider them as accents rather than a constant presence.

- **Loss of Flow:** If hiccups disrupt the natural flow of the rhythm, the overall groove may suffer. To maintain flow, practice playing or programming your hiccup sounds alongside your main beat until they feel like a natural part of the rhythm.

Examples of Hiccup Syncopation

To illustrate the concept of syncopation with hiccups, let's explore a few examples:

1. **Example 1: Basic Syncopation with Hiccups**

    Consider a simple drum pattern where the kick drum hits on beats 1 and 3, and the snare drum hits on beats 2 and 4. You can introduce hiccup sounds on the 'and' counts, creating a syncopated rhythm that feels lively and engaging.

2. **Example 2: Advanced Hiccup Syncopation**

    In a more complex example, imagine a drum pattern that incorporates hi-hats playing 16th notes. By placing hiccup sounds on the off-beats (the 'e' and 'a' counts), you can create a rich tapestry of rhythm that keeps listeners intrigued.

3. **Example 3: Layered Hiccups**

    You can layer hiccup sounds with different pitches or lengths over a steady beat. For example, use a short, sharp hiccup sound on the 'and' counts and a longer, breathy hiccup sound on the downbeats. This layering technique adds depth and complexity to your syncopated rhythm.

Conclusion

Syncopation is a powerful tool in hip hop, and when combined with the unexpected nature of hiccups, it can elevate your music to new heights. By understanding the principles of syncopation, experimenting with hiccup placement, and addressing common challenges, you can create unique rhythms that resonate with your audience. So go ahead, embrace the hiccups, and let them guide you to new creative territories in your hip hop journey!

Layering Hiccups with Percussion

Layering hiccups with percussion can elevate your hip hop tracks to new heights, creating a rich tapestry of sound that captures the listener's attention. In this section, we will explore the theory behind layering, the challenges you may encounter, and practical examples to help you effectively incorporate hiccups into your percussion arrangements.

Theoretical Foundations

Layering is a fundamental technique in music production that involves combining multiple sound elements to create a fuller, more complex auditory experience. In the context of hip hop, percussion serves as the backbone of a track, providing rhythm and energy. By introducing hiccups—unexpected, rhythmic interruptions—you can add a unique flavor to your beats.

The basic principle of layering is to ensure that each sound occupies its own frequency range. This can be achieved through careful selection of sounds and the use of equalization (EQ). Hiccups, typically characterized by short bursts of sound, can be layered with various percussion instruments like kick drums, snares, and hi-hats.

$$\text{Total Sound} = \text{Kick} + \text{Snare} + \text{Hi-Hat} + \text{Hiccups} \qquad (30)$$

In this equation, the total sound is a combination of the kick, snare, hi-hat, and hiccup elements. Each layer contributes to the overall texture of the track.

Challenges in Layering

While layering hiccups with percussion can yield exciting results, it also presents challenges. One common issue is phase cancellation, which occurs when two sound waves are out of alignment, resulting in a reduction of sound quality. To avoid this, it is essential to ensure that your hiccup samples are in phase with your percussion elements.

Another challenge is maintaining clarity in the mix. As you introduce more layers, it can become difficult to distinguish each sound. Here are some strategies to overcome these challenges:

- **Use EQ Wisely:** Apply EQ to carve out space for each sound. For instance, if your hiccup sample has a prominent mid-range frequency, you may want to reduce some of the mids in your kick or snare to prevent muddiness.

- **Adjust Levels:** Balance the volume levels of each layer. Hiccups should complement the percussion rather than overpower it. Start with the percussion elements at a comfortable level and then bring in the hiccups gradually.

HICCUP-INSPIRED DRUM PATTERNS

- **Experiment with Panning:** Use stereo panning to create width in your mix. For example, you can pan your kick and snare slightly to the left and right while keeping the hiccups centered, providing a sense of space.

Practical Examples

To illustrate how to effectively layer hiccups with percussion, let's consider a few practical examples:

Example 1: Hiccup-Infused Kick Drum Imagine a track where the kick drum has a strong presence. By layering hiccup samples that mimic the rhythm of the kick but are slightly delayed, you can create a syncopated groove. For instance, if your kick hits on beats 1 and 3, you could place hiccups on the "and" of 2 and 4, like so:

$$\text{Kick: } 1 \quad 2 \quad 3 \quad 4 \quad \text{Hiccups: } H \quad H \quad (31)$$

This technique creates an engaging interplay between the kick and hiccups, adding depth to the rhythm.

Example 2: Snare Layering In another scenario, consider layering hiccups with snare hits. If your snare has a sharp attack, you can use a hiccup sample that has a similar transient quality. Place the hiccup sample slightly before or after the snare hit to create a call-and-response effect. This can be particularly effective in creating tension and release in your track.

$$\text{Snare: } 1 \quad 2 \quad 3 \quad 4 \quad \text{Hiccups: } H \quad H \quad H \quad (32)$$

In this arrangement, the hiccups act as accents that enhance the snare's impact.

Example 3: Hi-Hat Variation Lastly, consider using hiccups to add variation to your hi-hat patterns. By layering hiccup samples at irregular intervals, you can create a more dynamic and unpredictable rhythm. For instance, if your hi-hat plays on every eighth note, you could place hiccups on the off-beats, creating an exciting syncopation.

$$\text{Hi-Hat: } 1 \ \& \ 2 \ \& \ 3 \ \& \ 4 \ \& \text{Hiccups: } H \quad H \quad H \quad (33)$$

This layering technique adds a playful element to your rhythm, keeping the listener engaged.

Conclusion

Layering hiccups with percussion is a powerful technique that can transform your hip hop tracks. By understanding the theoretical foundations, addressing potential challenges, and applying practical examples, you can create unique and captivating rhythms that stand out. Remember, the key is to experiment and find the right balance that works for your style. Embrace the hiccups, and let them inspire your creativity!

Creating Hiccup Grooves

Creating grooves that embody the essence of hiccups can transform your hip hop tracks into something truly unique and engaging. Hiccups, by their very nature, introduce unexpected pauses and shifts in rhythm that can be creatively harnessed to craft compelling beats. In this section, we will explore the theory behind hiccup grooves, the challenges they present, and practical examples to illustrate how you can implement them in your music.

Understanding Hiccup Grooves

At the core of hiccup grooves is the concept of syncopation. Syncopation occurs when a rhythmic pattern emphasizes beats or portions of beats that are typically not accented. This can create a feeling of surprise and tension, much like the unexpected nature of a hiccup.

Mathematically, a basic groove can be represented as a sequence of beats where the strong beats are typically on the downbeats (1 and 3 in a 4/4 measure). However, by introducing hiccup elements, we can shift some of these accents to offbeats or create irregular patterns.

For example, consider a simple 4/4 measure:

$$\text{Beat Pattern:} \quad 1 \quad 2 \quad 3 \quad 4$$

A basic groove might emphasize beats 1 and 3, creating a steady pulse. To incorporate hiccup grooves, we can introduce accents on the offbeats:

$$\text{Hiccup Groove:} \quad 1 \quad (h) \quad 3 \quad (h)$$

Where (h) represents a hiccup accent that disrupts the steady flow.

HICCUP-INSPIRED DRUM PATTERNS

Challenges in Creating Hiccup Grooves

While the idea of hiccup grooves is exciting, there are several challenges to consider:

1. **Maintaining Rhythm**: The primary challenge is to ensure that the groove remains danceable despite the irregularities introduced by hiccups. If the hiccup accents are too pronounced, they can confuse the listener and disrupt the flow of the track.

2. **Balancing Complexity and Accessibility**: Hiccup grooves can easily become overly complex, making it difficult for listeners to engage with the music. It's essential to strike a balance between innovative rhythms and the fundamental catchiness of hip hop.

3. **Integration with Other Elements**: Hiccup grooves should complement the other elements of your track, such as the bassline and melody. A hiccup groove that stands out too much can overshadow these components, leading to an unbalanced mix.

Practical Examples of Hiccup Grooves

To illustrate the concept of hiccup grooves, let's examine a few practical examples.

Example 1: Basic Hiccup Pattern Using a simple kick-snare pattern, we can create a hiccup groove by adding ghost notes (very soft notes) and emphasizing the hiccup accents.

- Kick: K   h   K   h
- Snare: S   S

In this example, K represents a kick drum, S represents a snare, and h represents a hiccup accent. The ghost notes (h) create a hiccup effect that adds complexity to the rhythm.

Example 2: Layering Hiccups with Percussion Another approach is to layer additional percussion elements to enhance the hiccup groove. Consider adding a hi-hat pattern that plays on the offbeats, creating a syncopated feel:

- Kick: K   h   K   h
- Snare: S   S
- Hi-Hat: h   h   h   h

Here, the hi-hat plays consistently while the kick and snare create the hiccup effect, resulting in a groove that feels lively and engaging.

Example 3: Creating Hiccup Grooves with MIDI   When working with MIDI, you can easily manipulate the timing of your notes to create hiccup grooves. For instance, you can shift the timing of certain notes slightly off the grid to create the hiccup effect.

Suppose you have a MIDI pattern set to quantize to 16th notes. By nudging some of the kick drum notes slightly ahead or behind their original positions, you can create a feeling of hiccups.

```
Original MIDI:    K  -  K  -  K  -  K
Hiccup MIDI:      K  -  -  K  -  K  -  K
```

In this example, the second kick is delayed, creating an unexpected hiccup that adds character to the groove.

Conclusion

Creating hiccup grooves is an innovative way to push the boundaries of hip hop music. By understanding the principles of syncopation, addressing the challenges of rhythm and complexity, and utilizing practical examples, you can effectively incorporate hiccup elements into your tracks. Remember, the key is to embrace the unpredictability of hiccups while ensuring that your groove remains accessible and engaging to your audience. So go ahead, make those hiccups work for you, and let your creativity flow!

Playful Hiccup Melodies

Pitch Variations that Mimic Hiccups

In the realm of hip hop music, pitch variations play a crucial role in creating unique and engaging sounds. One unconventional yet effective method to infuse creativity into your tracks is by mimicking the spontaneous nature of hiccups through pitch variations. This section will delve into the theory behind pitch variations, explore the problems that may arise when attempting to incorporate these techniques, and provide practical examples to inspire your music-making process.

Understanding Pitch Variations

Pitch variations refer to the deliberate changes in frequency of a sound over time. In music, pitch is typically measured in Hertz (Hz), which denotes the number of cycles per second of a sound wave. The human ear perceives these variations as changes in the tonal quality of the sound, influencing its emotional impact and overall character.

Incorporating pitch variations that mimic the unpredictable and abrupt nature of hiccups can add a playful and dynamic element to your compositions. Hiccups are characterized by a sudden intake of breath followed by a quick closure of the vocal cords, resulting in a distinct sound. This phenomenon can be translated into music through various techniques:

$$f(t) = A \sin(2\pi f_0 t + \phi) \tag{34}$$

where: - $f(t)$ is the sound wave function, - A is the amplitude, - f_0 is the frequency, - t is time, - ϕ is the phase shift.

By manipulating the amplitude A and frequency f_0 over time t, you can create pitch variations that echo the essence of hiccups.

Problems in Implementing Pitch Variations

While the idea of using pitch variations to mimic hiccups is innovative, several challenges may arise during the implementation process:

1. **Maintaining Musicality:** One of the primary concerns is ensuring that the pitch variations do not disrupt the overall musicality of the track. Overly abrupt changes can lead to dissonance, detracting from the listener's experience.

2. **Integrating with Other Elements:** Harmonizing pitch variations with beats, melodies, and lyrics can be complex. It requires a keen ear and an understanding of how different elements interact within the composition.

3. **Technical Limitations:** Depending on the software or hardware used for music production, there may be limitations in manipulating pitch in real-time. Understanding the capabilities of your tools is essential for successful implementation.

Examples of Pitch Variations in Hip Hop

To illustrate the effectiveness of pitch variations that mimic hiccups, consider the following examples:

1. **Vocal Samples:** Artists like *Busta Rhymes* and *Missy Elliott* have employed vocal samples that include hiccup-like sounds. By recording short vocal snippets

where the artist intentionally incorporates pitch variations, you can create a unique texture in your tracks.

2. **Synthesizers:** Utilizing synthesizers to create hiccup-inspired sounds can be achieved by modulating the pitch of a waveform. For instance, using a sawtooth wave and applying an LFO (Low-Frequency Oscillator) to modulate the pitch can produce a sound reminiscent of hiccups.

$$f_{\text{modulated}}(t) = A\sin(2\pi(f_0 + L \cdot \sin(2\pi f_{\text{LFO}}t))t) \tag{35}$$

where: - L is the modulation depth, - f_{LFO} is the frequency of the LFO.

3. **Drum Patterns:** Incorporating hiccup-like pitch variations in drum patterns can add an unexpected twist. For example, layering a kick drum with slight pitch modulation during specific beats can create a hiccup effect that engages the listener.

Practical Tips for Implementation

To effectively incorporate pitch variations that mimic hiccups into your hip hop tracks, consider the following tips:

- **Experiment with Automation:** Use automation in your digital audio workstation (DAW) to control pitch changes over time. This allows for precise manipulation of pitch variations, ensuring they fit seamlessly within your track.
- **Layer Sounds:** Combine multiple sounds with varying pitch to create a richer texture. For instance, layer a pitched-up vocal sample with a pitched-down synth to create contrast and depth.
- **Utilize Effects:** Employ effects such as pitch shifting, chorus, and reverb to enhance the hiccup-like quality of your sounds. Experimenting with different settings can yield unique results.
- **Record Live:** If possible, record live vocal performances where you intentionally incorporate hiccup-like pitch variations. This organic approach can add authenticity and character to your music.

In conclusion, pitch variations that mimic hiccups offer a fresh perspective on creativity in hip hop music. By understanding the underlying theory, addressing potential problems, and applying practical examples, you can elevate your compositions and engage your audience in new and exciting ways. Embrace the unpredictable nature of hiccups and let them inspire your musical journey.

Unconventional Intervals and Jumps

In the realm of music composition, particularly in hip hop, the use of unconventional intervals and jumps can elevate your sound, making it distinctive and memorable.

This section delves into the theory behind these musical elements, explores potential challenges, and provides examples to inspire your creative process.

Understanding Intervals

An interval is defined as the distance between two pitches. In Western music, intervals are typically categorized as major, minor, perfect, augmented, or diminished. The most common intervals used in popular music are the major third ($M3$) and the perfect fifth ($P5$). However, exploring unconventional intervals can lead to unique melodic structures that resonate with listeners in unexpected ways.

$$\text{Interval} = \text{Higher Pitch} - \text{Lower Pitch} \tag{36}$$

For example, the interval of a minor sixth ($m6$) can create a sense of tension and surprise. To play with this, a composer might move from a root note, say C, to an A-flat, which is a minor sixth above:

$$C \to A\flat \quad (m6) \tag{37}$$

Exploring Unconventional Jumps

Jumps, or leaps, occur when a melody skips over one or more notes. In hip hop, using larger leaps can create a dynamic and engaging sonic landscape. For instance, instead of following a stepwise motion (moving from one note to the adjacent note), consider jumping from a root note to a note several steps away, such as from C to E (a major third), or even further, like from C to G (a perfect fifth).

$$\text{Jump} = \text{Higher Note} - \text{Lower Note} \tag{38}$$

When composing, you might encounter challenges with leaps. Large jumps can disrupt the flow of a melody if not handled carefully. To mitigate this, you can use techniques like:

- **Passing Notes:** Insert transitional notes between leaps to create a smoother melodic line.

- **Rhythmic Variation:** Alter the rhythm around the leaps to maintain the listener's interest and provide a sense of movement.

Theoretical Implications

In music theory, unconventional intervals often evoke specific emotional responses. For example, the augmented fourth ($A4$) or diminished fifth ($d5$), commonly known as the tritone, can create a sense of tension or unease. This interval is famously used in the opening of "Maria" from *West Side Story*, which contributes to its dramatic effect.

In contrast, intervals such as the major seventh ($M7$) can evoke feelings of longing or resolution. Consider the jump from C to B:

$$C \to B \quad (M7) \tag{39}$$

Practical Examples

To illustrate the impact of unconventional intervals and jumps in hip hop, let's analyze a few notable tracks:

1. **Kendrick Lamar - "HUMBLE."** Lamar employs sharp, unexpected jumps in his vocal delivery, particularly in the chorus. The use of syncopation and leaps creates a sense of urgency, drawing the listener's attention.

2. **Missy Elliott - "Get Ur Freak On."** The track features intervals that blend traditional hip hop with world music influences. Elliott's use of the minor seventh interval gives her hooks a distinctive flavor, making them instantly recognizable.

3. **Childish Gambino - "Redbone."** The song utilizes unconventional intervals, notably the augmented fourth, creating a haunting atmosphere that complements the lyrical themes of betrayal and paranoia.

Creative Exercise

To practice incorporating unconventional intervals and jumps into your own music, try the following exercise:

1. Choose a root note (e.g., C).

2. Experiment with jumping to various intervals (e.g., $m6$, $A4$, $M7$).

3. Create a short melody using these jumps. Consider how the intervals affect the emotional tone of the melody.

4. Record your melody and listen back. Reflect on how the unconventional intervals contribute to the overall feel of the piece.

Conclusion

Incorporating unconventional intervals and jumps into your hip hop compositions can transform your music from ordinary to extraordinary. By understanding the theory behind these elements, recognizing potential challenges, and drawing inspiration from established artists, you can create unique sounds that resonate with your audience. Embrace the unpredictability of musical jumps, and let your creativity soar!

Quirky and Unconventional Compositions

In the realm of hip hop, creativity knows no bounds, and embracing the quirky and unconventional can lead to groundbreaking compositions. This section delves into the art of crafting unique musical pieces that defy traditional norms, using unexpected elements to create a fresh sound that resonates with listeners.

The Essence of Quirkiness in Composition

Quirkiness in music often stems from a willingness to break away from established patterns. It invites experimentation and the exploration of sounds that might initially seem out of place. In hip hop, this can be achieved through the use of unconventional instruments, unexpected time signatures, or unusual melodic structures. The goal is to surprise the listener and create a memorable experience.

For example, consider the track "B.O.B" by OutKast. The song features a rapid tempo and a blend of genres, including hip hop, rock, and funk. The unexpected shifts in rhythm and the incorporation of diverse musical elements create a composition that is both quirky and engaging.

Theoretical Foundations

To understand how to create quirky compositions, it's essential to grasp some fundamental music theory concepts. Here are a few key elements to consider:

- **Polyrhythms:** The simultaneous combination of contrasting rhythms can create a rich tapestry of sound. For instance, layering a 4/4 beat with a 3/4 rhythm can produce a compelling groove that keeps listeners on their toes. This technique can be effectively employed in hip hop beats to add depth and complexity.

- **Non-Traditional Scales:** Experimenting with scales outside the typical major and minor can yield surprising results. The use of the *whole tone scale* or *pentatonic scale* can evoke a unique atmosphere. For instance, the use of the Dorian mode can impart a jazzy feel that contrasts with standard hip hop melodies.

- **Unexpected Harmonic Progressions:** Traditional chord progressions often follow predictable patterns (e.g., I-IV-V). However, incorporating unexpected changes, such as modulating to a different key or utilizing diminished chords, can create a sense of surprise and intrigue. Consider the use of the *circle of fifths* to create tension and resolution in your compositions.

Practical Applications

To apply these theoretical concepts in your compositions, consider the following techniques:

1. **Layering Sounds:** Begin by layering different sounds and rhythms. For instance, you might combine a traditional hip hop drum pattern with a jazz piano riff. This juxtaposition can create an engaging contrast that captures the listener's attention.

2. **Incorporating Unconventional Instruments:** Experiment with instruments that are not typically associated with hip hop, such as ukuleles, theremins, or even household items like pots and pans. The incorporation of these sounds can add a playful element to your tracks.

3. **Play with Structure:** Challenge the conventional structure of a song (verse-chorus-verse) by introducing unexpected breaks or interludes. For example, a sudden spoken word section or a brief instrumental break can create a refreshing shift in the composition.

Case Studies

Let's explore a couple of notable examples of quirky and unconventional hip hop compositions:

1. *"Psycho" by Post Malone featuring Ty Dolla $ign* This track showcases an unusual blend of hip hop and rock elements, with a catchy chorus that incorporates a sing-along quality. The use of distorted guitar riffs alongside traditional hip hop beats creates a unique sound that stands out in the genre.

PLAYFUL HICCUP MELODIES

2. "*Feel Good Inc.*" by Gorillaz   While not strictly hip hop, this song incorporates hip hop influences and features a quirky composition. The use of a catchy bassline, layered vocals, and unconventional sound effects creates a surreal listening experience that blurs genre boundaries.

Challenges and Solutions

Creating quirky compositions can pose challenges, particularly in maintaining coherence and ensuring that the unconventional elements enhance rather than detract from the overall sound. Here are some common problems and potential solutions:

- **Problem: Loss of Cohesion**
  Solution: Establish a clear theme or concept for your track. Even if the sounds are unconventional, a strong thematic foundation can help unify the composition.

- **Problem: Overwhelming Complexity**
  Solution: Balance complexity with simplicity. While it's essential to experiment, ensure that the listener can still engage with the core elements of the track.

- **Problem: Alienating Your Audience**
  Solution: Test your compositions with a small audience. Gather feedback to gauge whether the quirkiness resonates or if adjustments are needed to make the track more accessible.

Conclusion

Incorporating quirky and unconventional elements into your hip hop compositions can lead to innovative and memorable music. By embracing experimentation, understanding music theory, and learning from successful examples, you can develop a unique sound that sets you apart in the industry. Remember, the beauty of hip hop lies in its diversity and ability to evolve, so don't be afraid to let your creativity run wild. The next time you sit down to create, consider how you can inject a bit of quirkiness into your work—your audience will thank you for it!

Sampling Hiccups in Your Beats

Finding Unique Hiccup Sounds to Sample

In the world of Hip Hop production, sampling is an art form that breathes new life into sounds, transforming the ordinary into the extraordinary. When it comes to incorporating hiccup sounds into your tracks, the challenge lies in finding unique and creative ways to capture these fleeting moments. This section will explore techniques for discovering and utilizing hiccup sounds that can elevate your music to new heights.

Understanding Hiccups as Sound

Hiccups are involuntary contractions of the diaphragm, followed by a sudden closure of the vocal cords, which produces the characteristic "hic" sound. This sound can vary in pitch, duration, and intensity, making it an intriguing candidate for sampling. To effectively sample hiccup sounds, it is essential to understand their acoustic properties.

The general waveform of a hiccup can be modeled as a short impulse followed by a decay. Mathematically, this can be represented by the equation:

$$y(t) = A \cdot e^{-\frac{t}{\tau}} \cdot \sin(2\pi f t) \tag{40}$$

where:

- $y(t)$ is the amplitude of the sound wave at time t,
- A is the peak amplitude,
- τ is the time constant that determines the decay,
- f is the frequency of the sound wave.

This equation indicates that the hiccup sound has a fast attack and a quick decay, making it a percussive element that can fit seamlessly into various musical contexts.

Recording Techniques

To capture unique hiccup sounds, consider the following recording techniques:

- **Microphone Selection:** Use a high-quality condenser microphone to capture the nuances of the hiccup sound. The sensitivity of condenser mics can pick up subtle variations in the sound that dynamic mics may miss.

SAMPLING HICCUPS IN YOUR BEATS 73

- **Recording Environment:** Create a controlled recording environment. A quiet room with minimal background noise will ensure that the hiccup sounds are clear and distinct. Consider using soundproofing materials to minimize external noise.

- **Multiple Takes:** Record multiple takes of hiccup sounds. Encourage the subject to vary the intensity, pitch, and rhythm of their hiccups. This will provide a diverse collection of samples to choose from during the production process.

Creative Sampling Techniques

Once you have recorded a variety of hiccup sounds, the next step is to manipulate and incorporate them into your tracks. Here are some creative sampling techniques:

- **Time Stretching:** Use time-stretching techniques to alter the duration of the hiccup sound without affecting its pitch. This can create elongated hiccup sounds that can serve as atmospheric elements in your production.

- **Pitch Shifting:** Experiment with pitch shifting to create harmonies or counterpoints with the original hiccup sounds. By raising or lowering the pitch, you can create a unique sonic palette that adds depth to your tracks.

- **Layering:** Layer multiple hiccup sounds to create a more complex texture. By combining different pitches and intensities, you can create a rhythmic foundation that drives the track forward.

Examples of Hiccup Sampling in Hip Hop

Several artists have successfully incorporated unique sounds into their music, demonstrating the potential of sampling hiccup sounds:

- **Kanye West:** In his track "Stronger," Kanye samples Daft Punk's "Harder, Better, Faster, Stronger," which features robotic vocal samples. Imagine layering a hiccup sound in a similar fashion to create a unique rhythmic element.

- **Missy Elliott:** Known for her innovative use of sound, Missy Elliott often incorporates unconventional samples. A hiccup sample could be woven into her tracks to add an unexpected twist, enhancing the playful nature of her music.

- **Anderson .Paak:** His blend of hip hop and R&B often features unique vocal samples. By sampling hiccups, you can achieve a quirky yet infectious groove reminiscent of his style.

Ethical Considerations in Sampling

When sampling any sound, including hiccups, it is crucial to consider the ethical implications. Always ensure that you have the necessary permissions to use recorded sounds, especially if they feature identifiable individuals. Clear any samples you intend to use in commercial releases to avoid legal complications.

Conclusion

Finding unique hiccup sounds to sample can open up a world of creative possibilities in your Hip Hop productions. By understanding the acoustic properties of hiccups, employing effective recording techniques, and exploring innovative sampling methods, you can transform these seemingly mundane sounds into powerful musical elements. Embrace the quirks of hiccups and let them inspire your next track, proving that imperfections can lead to extraordinary artistry.

Chopping and Manipulating Hiccup Samples

Chopping and manipulating hiccup samples is a creative technique that allows you to infuse your hip hop tracks with unique sounds and rhythms. This section will explore the theory behind sample manipulation, common problems you may encounter, and examples to inspire your own creations.

The Theory of Sample Manipulation

Sampling is a fundamental aspect of hip hop production, where producers take snippets of existing recordings and recontextualize them within a new composition. When it comes to hiccup samples, the goal is to transform these sounds into rhythmic and melodic elements that enhance your track. The manipulation process can involve several techniques, including:

- **Chopping:** This involves cutting the sample into smaller pieces to rearrange them in a way that creates new rhythms or patterns.
- **Time Stretching:** Altering the playback speed of the sample without affecting its pitch. This can create interesting variations of the hiccup sound.

SAMPLING HICCUPS IN YOUR BEATS

- **Pitch Shifting:** Changing the pitch of the sample up or down, allowing you to create harmonies or counterpoints.

- **Layering:** Combining multiple samples together to create a fuller sound, which can add depth and complexity to your track.

The mathematical representation of sample manipulation can be illustrated through the following equation, which describes the relationship between time, frequency, and pitch:

$$f(t) = A \cdot \sin(2\pi f_0 t + \phi) \qquad (41)$$

Where:

- $f(t)$ is the sound wave function,
- A is the amplitude (volume),
- f_0 is the frequency (pitch),
- t is time,
- ϕ is the phase shift.

By manipulating the parameters of this equation, producers can create a variety of effects that breathe new life into hiccup samples.

Common Problems in Sample Manipulation

While chopping and manipulating hiccup samples can yield exciting results, it is not without its challenges. Here are some common problems you may encounter:

- **Timing Issues:** When chopping samples, it is crucial to maintain the groove of the original beat. If the timing is off, the rhythm can feel disjointed. Consider using a metronome or a digital audio workstation (DAW) with a quantization feature to align your samples properly.

- **Phase Cancellation:** When layering multiple samples, certain frequencies may cancel each other out, resulting in a thin sound. This can be mitigated by adjusting the phase of the samples or using EQ to carve out space for each sound.

- **Loss of Quality:** Over-manipulating a sample can lead to artifacts or a loss of audio quality. It's essential to find a balance between creativity and preserving the integrity of the original sound.

Examples of Hiccup Sample Manipulation

To illustrate the techniques discussed, let's explore some practical examples of how to chop and manipulate hiccup samples effectively:

- **Chopping for Rhythm:** Take a short hiccup sound and chop it into four equal parts. Rearrange these parts to create a syncopated rhythm. For instance, if the original hiccup is recorded in 4/4 time, you can place the first and third chops on the downbeat and the second and fourth chops on the upbeat to create a staggered effect.

- **Time Stretching for Variation:** Use time stretching to elongate a hiccup sample to create a drawn-out sound that can serve as a pad or atmospheric element in your track. This technique works particularly well when combined with reverb to create a lush background sound.

- **Pitch Shifting for Melodic Elements:** Experiment with pitch shifting by raising the pitch of a hiccup sound by a third or a fifth. This can transform the hiccup into a melodic hook that complements your main beat.

- **Layering for Depth:** Layer different hiccup samples together, adjusting their volume levels and panning to create a rich, textured sound. For example, you might layer a high-pitched hiccup sample with a low-pitched one, creating a contrast that adds complexity to your track.

Conclusion

Chopping and manipulating hiccup samples is an innovative way to enhance your hip hop productions. By understanding the theory behind sample manipulation, recognizing common challenges, and applying practical techniques, you can create unique sounds that set your music apart. Remember, the key is to experiment and embrace the unexpected outcomes that arise from using hiccup samples in your work. With practice, you'll find that these techniques not only enrich your sound but also inspire your creative process.

Applying Hiccups Creatively in Your Tracks

In the vibrant world of Hip Hop, creativity knows no bounds. One of the most unexpected sources of inspiration can come from something as trivial as a hiccup. This section delves into the art of incorporating hiccups into your tracks, transforming an involuntary reflex into a powerful creative tool.

SAMPLING HICCUPS IN YOUR BEATS

Understanding the Hiccup as a Musical Element

Hiccups can be understood as rhythmic interruptions in a flow, akin to syncopation in music. To apply hiccups creatively, consider them as a musical element that can enhance the texture and dynamics of your tracks. The hiccup can be represented mathematically in terms of rhythm:

$$R = \{t_1, t_2, t_3, \ldots, t_n\} \qquad (42)$$

where R is the rhythm pattern, and t_i represents the time intervals between beats. By introducing hiccups, you can create irregularities in t_i that add a layer of unpredictability.

Incorporating Hiccups into Beats

To effectively incorporate hiccups into your beats, consider the following approaches:

- **Sample Hiccups:** Record natural hiccup sounds and manipulate them. You can chop, stretch, or pitch-shift these samples to create unique percussive elements. For instance, a hiccup can be layered over a kick drum to create a distinctive sound that stands out in the mix.

- **Hiccup Breaks:** Use hiccup sounds as breaks within your track. These breaks can serve as a transition between sections, providing a moment of surprise and engaging listeners. For example, after a verse, introduce a hiccup break before launching into the chorus, creating anticipation.

- **Dynamic Rhythm Shifts:** Utilize hiccups to shift the dynamics of your track. By strategically placing hiccup samples in quieter sections, you can elevate the energy when transitioning to more intense parts of the song. This technique can be particularly effective in building tension before a drop.

Creative Use of Hiccups in Melody

Hiccups can also inspire melodic creativity. Consider the following methods to apply hiccups in your melodic lines:

- **Pitch Bends:** Use pitch bends to mimic the sound of a hiccup. This technique can be applied to synthesizers or vocal lines, creating a quirky, playful sound. For instance, a rising pitch followed by a quick drop can evoke the essence of a hiccup, adding character to your melodies.

- **Rhythmic Variation:** Introduce hiccup-like rhythms in your melodic phrases. By incorporating unexpected pauses or syncopated notes, you can create a sense of movement and excitement. This can be achieved by altering the note lengths within a phrase, creating a hiccup effect that keeps listeners engaged.

- **Layering Textures:** Layer multiple melodic lines that incorporate hiccup-inspired rhythms. This can create a rich tapestry of sound, where each layer contributes to the overall hiccup motif. Experiment with different instruments to see how they interact with the hiccup elements.

Case Studies and Examples

To illustrate the application of hiccups in Hip Hop tracks, let's examine a few notable examples:

- **"Hiccup Bounce" by DJ Quik:** In this track, DJ Quik uses a sampled hiccup layered with a heavy bassline. The hiccup acts as a rhythmic accent, enhancing the groove and making the track more danceable. The unexpected nature of the hiccup keeps the listener engaged.

- **"Hiccups and Rhymes" by Chance the Rapper:** Chance creatively incorporates hiccup sounds into his vocal delivery. He uses hiccup-like pauses to create tension in his verses, leading to powerful punchlines. This technique not only adds a unique flavor to his flow but also emphasizes key lyrical moments.

- **"Unexpected Turns" by Anderson .Paak:** In this song, Anderson .Paak employs hiccup-inspired breaks between verses. The hiccups serve as a playful interlude, allowing the listener to catch their breath before diving back into the lyrical flow. This technique showcases the versatility of hiccups as a structural element in music.

Challenges and Considerations

While incorporating hiccups into your tracks can be a source of innovation, there are challenges to consider:

- **Balancing Complexity:** It's essential to balance the complexity of hiccup elements with the overall flow of your track. Overusing hiccups can lead to a chaotic sound that detracts from the main melody or message.

- **Mixing and EQ:** Hiccups can introduce unexpected frequencies that may clash with other elements in your mix. Pay attention to the EQ and ensure that hiccup samples sit well within the overall frequency spectrum.

- **Audience Reception:** Not all listeners may appreciate the incorporation of hiccups. It's crucial to gauge your audience's response and adapt your approach accordingly. Experimentation is key, but so is understanding your listener's preferences.

Conclusion

In conclusion, applying hiccups creatively in your Hip Hop tracks can lead to innovative sounds and engaging rhythms. By embracing the unpredictability of hiccups, you can transform a simple bodily function into a powerful artistic tool. Whether through sampling, melodic variation, or dynamic shifts, the incorporation of hiccups can help define your unique sound and keep your audience captivated. Remember, the essence of Hip Hop lies in its ability to break conventions—so why not let a little hiccup be part of your musical journey?

Perfecting Hiccup-Friendly Rhymes

Embracing Hiccup-Induced Pauses in Your Flow

Using Hiccups as Natural Breaks

In the world of hip hop, rhythm is everything. The flow of your lyrics, the beats that underpin your verses, and the pauses that punctuate your performance all contribute to the overall experience of your music. One often overlooked yet powerful tool in achieving this rhythmic mastery is the use of hiccups as natural breaks. This section explores how to effectively incorporate hiccups into your flow, creating dynamic pauses that enhance the storytelling aspect of your lyrics.

Theoretical Foundation

Hiccups, while often seen as an annoyance, can serve as a unique rhythmic device. In music theory, rests are as crucial as notes; they provide space for the listener to absorb what has been said and anticipate what comes next. Hiccups can function similarly, acting as unexpected rests that disrupt the flow in a way that captivates the audience's attention.

Mathematically, if we consider the structure of a bar in 4/4 time, we can represent the flow of lyrics and hiccups as follows:

$$\text{Flow} = \text{Note} + \text{Hiccup} + \text{Note} \tag{43}$$

This equation illustrates how a hiccup can be integrated into the flow, serving as a bridge between two lyrical phrases. The hiccup creates a momentary pause that adds emphasis to the words that precede and follow it.

Problems with Traditional Flow

Many aspiring hip hop artists struggle with maintaining a consistent flow. They often adhere strictly to rhythmic patterns, which can lead to predictability in their delivery. This rigidity can make their music feel flat and unengaging. By incorporating hiccups, artists can break free from these constraints, allowing for a more organic and spontaneous performance.

Consider the following common problems:

- **Monotony:** A consistent flow without variation can lead to listener fatigue.
- **Lack of Emotion:** Without pauses, the emotional weight of the lyrics may be lost.
- **Missed Opportunities:** Failing to incorporate natural breaks can result in a lack of dramatic tension in storytelling.

By embracing hiccups as natural breaks, artists can address these issues, introducing an element of surprise and enhancing emotional impact.

Examples of Hiccup Integration

Let's analyze some examples of how hiccups can be effectively integrated into hip hop lyrics:

1. **Example 1: Kendrick Lamar's "HUMBLE."** In this track, Kendrick uses hiccup-like pauses to emphasize his confidence and command over the beat. The hiccups create a staccato effect that punctuates his assertive lyrics, making each line hit harder.

> "Get the f*** off my stage, I'm the Sandman (Hiccup) / Get the f*** off my stage, I'm the Sandman."

Here, the hiccup serves as a natural break, enhancing the intensity of his delivery and allowing the audience to absorb the weight of his words.

2. **Example 2: Chance the Rapper's "No Problem."** Chance often incorporates playful hiccup-like breaks in his flow, which add a layer of fun and spontaneity to his verses.

> "If one more label try to stop me (Hiccup) / It's gon' be some dreadhead n****s in your lobby."

The hiccup before "It's gon' be" creates a moment of anticipation, making the punchline more impactful.

Practical Techniques for Implementation

To effectively use hiccups as natural breaks in your flow, consider the following techniques:

1. **Experiment with Timing:** Play around with the placement of hiccups within your verses. Try inserting them at different points to see how they change the feel of your delivery.

2. **Use Breath Control:** Practice controlling your breath to create hiccup-like pauses. This can be achieved through vocal exercises that focus on breath support and control.

3. **Record and Analyze:** Record your verses and listen back to identify where hiccups can enhance your flow. This self-analysis can help you pinpoint areas where a natural break could add value.

Conclusion

Incorporating hiccups as natural breaks in your hip hop flow can transform your music, making it more engaging and dynamic. By embracing these unexpected pauses, you not only enhance your rhythmic delivery but also create space for emotional resonance and storytelling. So, the next time you sit down to write, remember that a well-placed hiccup might just be the secret ingredient to taking your lyrics to the next level.

Incorporating Hiccup Rhythms into Your Delivery

In the realm of Hip Hop, rhythm is the heartbeat of the music, and every artist must find their unique pulse. When we talk about incorporating hiccup rhythms into your delivery, we delve into the fascinating interplay between unexpected pauses and the flow of your lyrics. Hiccups, often seen as interruptions, can actually serve as powerful tools to enhance your performance and engage your audience.

Understanding Hiccup Rhythms

Hiccups are involuntary contractions of the diaphragm, often leading to a characteristic sound. In music, we can mimic this phenomenon by introducing rhythmic pauses that disrupt the expected flow. This technique can create a dynamic listening experience, drawing attention to specific words or phrases.

Mathematically, we can represent a hiccup rhythm using the concept of syncopation, where the emphasis shifts away from the expected beats. If we denote a steady beat as B, a hiccup can be introduced as an off-beat pause P such that:

$$R(t) = B(t) + P(t)$$

where $R(t)$ is the resultant rhythm at time t, $B(t)$ is the regular beat, and $P(t)$ is the hiccup pause. The integration of $P(t)$ can create a unique rhythmic signature, allowing your delivery to stand out.

Theoretical Foundations

Theoretical frameworks in music often explore the concepts of timing, phrasing, and rhythm. According to the principles of rhythm theory, incorporating unexpected rhythms can lead to a heightened sense of tension and release, essential elements in storytelling through music.

Practical Application

Incorporating hiccup rhythms into your delivery involves practice and experimentation. Here are some techniques to effectively integrate these rhythms:

- **Vocal Exercises:** Begin by practicing your lyrics with intentional hiccups. For example, recite a line and insert a hiccup after certain words to see how it changes the flow.

- **Recording and Playback:** Record yourself delivering verses with varying hiccup placements. Playback the recordings to analyze how the hiccups affect the overall rhythm and emotional tone.

- **Collaborative Jam Sessions:** Work with fellow artists to explore hiccup rhythms in a live setting. Freestyle sessions can lead to spontaneous and innovative uses of rhythm.

Common Challenges

While incorporating hiccup rhythms can be creatively liberating, it also presents challenges. Some artists may struggle with maintaining a consistent flow while introducing pauses. Here are common problems and solutions:

EMBRACING HICCUP-INDUCED PAUSES IN YOUR FLOW

- **Loss of Flow:** Hiccups can disrupt the flow of your delivery. To counter this, practice your verses slowly, gradually increasing speed while maintaining hiccup placements.

- **Audience Confusion:** If hiccups are used excessively or without clear intention, they may confuse listeners. Aim for balance; use hiccups to emphasize key moments rather than as a constant feature.

- **Timing Issues:** Improper timing of hiccups can lead to awkward breaks. Use a metronome during practice to develop a sense of timing that feels natural and engaging.

Examples of Hiccup Rhythms in Hip Hop

Many successful Hip Hop artists have utilized hiccup rhythms in their delivery. For instance, consider the work of artists like *Eminem* and *Busta Rhymes*, who often play with rhythm and timing in their verses.

In Eminem's track "Rap God," he employs rapid-fire delivery punctuated by strategic pauses, creating a hiccup-like effect that heightens the intensity of his message. Analyzing such tracks can provide valuable insights into how to effectively incorporate hiccup rhythms into your own style.

Another example is *Anderson .Paak*, who often blends rhythm and melody with playful hiccup-like inflections in his delivery. His ability to seamlessly integrate these rhythms showcases the potential for hiccups to enhance musicality while maintaining lyrical integrity.

Conclusion

Incorporating hiccup rhythms into your delivery is not just about adding pauses; it's about reimagining the way you approach rhythm in Hip Hop. By embracing these unexpected interruptions, you can create a unique sound that resonates with your audience. Remember, the beauty of Hip Hop lies in its ability to evolve and adapt, so don't shy away from experimenting with hiccup rhythms in your music. With practice and creativity, you can transform what may seem like a flaw into a defining feature of your artistic expression.

Experimenting with Rhyme Schemes for Hiccups

In the vibrant world of hip hop, rhyme schemes are the backbone of lyrical creativity. When it comes to incorporating hiccups into your flow, experimenting with various rhyme schemes can transform the ordinary into the extraordinary. This section delves into how to weave hiccups into your rhymes, creating a unique sonic experience that resonates with your audience.

Understanding Rhyme Schemes

Rhyme schemes refer to the pattern of rhymes at the end of each line in a verse. Common schemes include:

- **AABB**: Two consecutive lines rhyme with each other.
- **ABAB**: Alternate lines rhyme.
- **ABBA**: The first and fourth lines rhyme, as do the second and third.
- **ABCABC**: A more complex structure where the first three lines and the second three lines rhyme in a repeating pattern.

Understanding these schemes is crucial, as they provide a framework that can be manipulated to accommodate hiccups.

The Role of Hiccups in Rhyme Schemes

Hiccups, when infused into your lyrical delivery, can create unexpected pauses that add a layer of complexity to your rhyme schemes. These interruptions can serve as natural breaks, allowing you to play with rhythm and pacing. The key is to embrace these hiccups as part of your lyrical identity rather than viewing them as obstacles.

Problems and Solutions

Problem 1: Maintaining Flow One challenge that arises when incorporating hiccups is maintaining the flow of your lyrics. A sudden pause can disrupt the rhythm, making it difficult for listeners to follow along.

Solution: Strategic Placement To overcome this, experiment with placing hiccups at strategic points within your rhyme scheme. For example, if you are using an AABB scheme, you might place a hiccup at the end of the first line, allowing the second line to flow smoothly:

> I'm spitting bars, they're feeling *(hiccup)* fresh,
> Rhymes so tight, they're bound to impress.

Here, the hiccup adds a playful element without sacrificing the overall rhythm.

Problem 2: Altered Rhyme Patterns   Another issue is that hiccups can alter the expected rhyme patterns, leading to potential dissonance in your lyrics.

Solution: Embrace Dissonance   Instead of shying away from this dissonance, lean into it. Use it to your advantage by creating a new rhyme scheme that reflects the unpredictability of hiccups. For instance, you could modify an ABAB scheme to include a hiccup, resulting in a unique pattern:

> I'm on the grind, making moves *(hiccup)* so slick,
> Haters gonna hate, but I'm quick
> With every line, I'm bound to be *(hiccup)* the pick,
> Spitting truth, that's my trick.

This approach not only maintains the integrity of your rhyme scheme but also highlights the hiccup as a distinct feature of your delivery.

Examples of Hiccup-Infused Rhyme Schemes

To further illustrate the concept, let's explore some examples of how to integrate hiccups into different rhyme schemes:

Example 1: AABB Scheme

> Life's a journey, I'm taking *(hiccup)* flight,
> Chasing dreams, shining *(hiccup)* bright.

In this example, the hiccup adds a moment of hesitation that emphasizes the theme of pursuit.

Example 2: ABAB Scheme

> Beats drop heavy, I'm feeling *(hiccup)* bold,
> Words like fire, they're hot *(hiccup)* and cold.

Here, the hiccup creates a contrast that mirrors the duality of the lyrics.

Example 3: ABCABC Scheme

> In the city lights, I'm chasing *(hiccup)* dreams,
> With every step, I'm breaking *(hiccup)* seams,
> Rhymes so fresh, they flow *(hiccup)* like streams.

This example showcases how hiccups can enhance a more complex rhyme scheme, adding depth and texture.

Conclusion

Experimenting with rhyme schemes while incorporating hiccups can lead to a distinctive style that sets you apart in the hip hop landscape. Embrace the unexpected nature of hiccups and let them inform your lyrical choices. Remember, the beauty of hip hop lies in its ability to adapt and evolve, and your hiccup-infused rhymes are a testament to this creative spirit. So, get out there, play with your words, and let your hiccups shine!

Storytelling with Hiccups

Adding Emotion with Hiccups

In the realm of hip hop, emotion is the heartbeat of every track. It's what makes a listener connect, feel, and sometimes even cry. Hiccups, often perceived as mere interruptions, can actually serve as powerful emotional tools in your lyrical arsenal. In this section, we will explore how to harness the unpredictable nature of hiccups to convey deep emotions, enhance storytelling, and create a unique listening experience.

Understanding the Emotional Impact of Hiccups

Hiccups are involuntary contractions of the diaphragm, often resulting in a distinctive sound that can be both jarring and amusing. However, when incorporated into hip hop, they can evoke a variety of emotional responses. The key lies in the timing, delivery, and context of the hiccup within your lyrics.

Consider the following emotional theories that can be applied to the use of hiccups in hip hop:

- **Affective Priming:** This theory suggests that exposure to one stimulus influences the response to another stimulus. A hiccup can serve as a cue that

STORYTELLING WITH HICCUPS 89

primes the listener's emotional state, enhancing the impact of the subsequent lyrics.

- **Incongruity Theory:** Hiccups introduce an element of surprise or incongruity that can provoke laughter or discomfort, depending on the context. This can be strategically used to shift the emotional tone of a track.

- **Embodied Emotion:** The physicality of a hiccup can mirror the physical sensations of emotion, such as excitement or anxiety. This connection can deepen the listener's emotional engagement.

Crafting Emotionally Charged Lyrics with Hiccups

To effectively add emotion to your hip hop tracks using hiccups, consider the following techniques:

1. **Timing is Everything** The placement of a hiccup within your flow can dramatically alter the emotional weight of your lyrics. For instance, inserting a hiccup right before a poignant line can heighten anticipation and draw the listener in.

$$\text{Emotional Impact} = \text{Hiccup Timing} \times \text{Lyrical Weight} \qquad (44)$$

2. **Contrast and Juxtaposition** Utilize hiccups to create contrasts in your verses. For example, a smooth, flowing line can be disrupted by a hiccup, emphasizing a sudden emotional shift—be it joy, sorrow, or anger.

$$\text{Emotional Contrast} = \text{Flow Smoothness} - \text{Hiccup Interruption} \qquad (45)$$

3. **Storytelling with Hiccups** Incorporate hiccups into your narrative structure. For example, if you're telling a story of heartbreak, a hiccup can symbolize a moment of vulnerability, a break in composure.

> "I thought we had it all, but then you walked away, hiccup—just like that, my world went gray."

This line illustrates how a hiccup can punctuate the emotional weight of the narrative, making the moment more relatable and impactful.

Examples of Emotionally Charged Hiccup Usage

To illustrate the effectiveness of hiccups in conveying emotion, let's analyze a few examples from notable hip hop tracks:

Example 1: In a track that discusses loss, the artist uses a hiccup after the line, "I can't breathe without you, hiccup—my heart's in pieces." The hiccup here serves as a physical manifestation of the artist's grief, making the listener feel the weight of the moment.

Example 2: In a more upbeat track, an artist might incorporate a hiccup after a punchline, such as, "I'm rising to the top, hiccup—can't stop, won't drop!" This playful use of hiccups injects humor and lightness into the flow, enhancing the track's overall vibe.

Challenges and Considerations

While incorporating hiccups can enhance emotional expression, there are challenges to consider:

- **Overuse:** Too many hiccups can disrupt the flow and distract the listener. It's essential to use them judiciously.

- **Contextual Relevance:** Ensure that the use of hiccups aligns with the emotional tone of the track. A hiccup in a serious context may come off as inappropriate or comedic rather than poignant.

- **Audience Reception:** Be mindful of how your audience may perceive the use of hiccups. What resonates with one listener may not resonate with another.

Conclusion

Incorporating hiccups into your hip hop lyrics is not just about adding a quirky element; it's about leveraging the emotional potential of these interruptions. By understanding the emotional theories behind hiccups and employing them strategically in your storytelling, you can create a more profound connection with your audience. Remember, the goal is to embrace the unpredictability of hiccups and transform them into an integral part of your lyrical identity. So next time you feel a hiccup coming on, don't shy away—let it inspire your next verse!

Bringing Humor to Your Hiccup Tales

Humor is a powerful tool in storytelling, especially within the realm of hip hop, where authenticity and relatability reign supreme. When it comes to incorporating hiccups into your lyrics, the unexpected nature of these little interruptions can lead to comedic gold. This section will explore how to effectively weave humor into your hiccup tales, creating a memorable and engaging experience for your listeners.

The Role of Humor in Hip Hop

Humor serves multiple purposes in hip hop. It can break tension, foster connection, and provide a unique lens through which listeners can engage with serious topics. Artists like **Lil Dicky** and **Weird Al Yankovic** exemplify how humor can be used to create catchy and entertaining tracks while still addressing relevant themes. When you introduce hiccups into your narratives, you add an element of surprise that can amplify the comedic effect.

Crafting Hiccup Humor

To effectively bring humor into your hiccup tales, consider the following strategies:

- **Exaggeration:** Amplifying the absurdity of a situation can enhance its comedic value. For example, if you're rapping about a date gone wrong, you might describe how your hiccups caused you to accidentally spit out your drink, leading to an awkward yet hilarious moment.

- **Wordplay:** Utilize puns and clever language to create humorous connections between hiccups and your subject matter. For instance, you could play with the word "hick-up" as a metaphor for a setback or challenge in your life, turning a physical hiccup into a relatable life lesson.

- **Timing:** Just as in stand-up comedy, timing is crucial in hip hop. Use pauses effectively to let the audience absorb the humor of a hiccup moment. A well-placed hiccup can serve as a punchline, catching listeners off guard and eliciting laughter.

Examples of Hiccup Humor in Lyrics

Let's examine a few examples of how to incorporate humor into your lyrics through hiccups:

> "I walked into the club, feeling all fly,
> But then a hiccup hit, and I lost my cool, oh my!
> Spilled my drink on the floor, made the crowd go wild,
> They laughed so hard, thought I was just a child."

In this example, the hiccup serves as a catalyst for a humorous scenario, showcasing the artist's ability to turn an embarrassing moment into entertainment.

Theoretical Framework: The Incongruity Theory of Humor

The Incongruity Theory posits that humor arises when there is a discrepancy between what is expected and what actually occurs. This theory can be applied to hiccup humor in the following ways:

$$H = E - A \qquad (46)$$

Where:

- H = Humor
- E = Expectation (what the audience anticipates)
- A = Actual outcome (the unexpected hiccup)

In the context of hip hop, listeners expect a smooth flow and rhythmic delivery. When a hiccup disrupts this flow, it creates an incongruity that can lead to laughter, provided it is executed effectively.

Common Pitfalls to Avoid

While humor can enhance your lyrics, there are some pitfalls to be aware of:

- **Overdoing It:** Too many hiccup jokes can dilute their impact. Use them sparingly to maintain their effectiveness.
- **Inappropriate Context:** Ensure that the humor aligns with the overall theme of your song. Inappropriate humor can alienate listeners.
- **Neglecting Emotion:** While humor is important, don't forget to balance it with emotional depth. The best hip hop often combines humor with poignant themes.

Conclusion

Bringing humor into your hiccup tales not only makes your lyrics more engaging but also allows you to connect with your audience on a deeper level. By leveraging exaggeration, wordplay, and timing, you can create memorable and relatable stories that resonate with listeners. Remember, the key to successful hiccup humor lies in its unexpectedness, so embrace the quirks and let your creativity flow. With practice, your hiccup-infused tales can become a signature element of your hip hop style, leaving your audience laughing and wanting more.

Relatability through Hiccup Narratives

In the world of hip hop, storytelling is not just an art; it is the very essence of the genre. When we talk about **relatability**, we refer to the ability of the artist to connect with their audience on a personal level. This connection can be heightened through the incorporation of *hiccup narratives*—tales that resonate with the listener's experiences and emotions, often infused with the quirks of life that we all encounter.

The Power of Personal Stories

Every artist has a unique story to tell, and these narratives often include moments of vulnerability, struggle, and triumph. Hiccups, both literal and metaphorical, serve as a powerful metaphor for the unpredictable nature of life. They remind us that imperfections are a shared human experience. By weaving hiccup narratives into their lyrics, artists can create a tapestry of authenticity that resonates deeply with listeners.

For instance, consider the lyrics of *"Hiccup Blues"* by a contemporary artist. The track narrates a series of embarrassing moments that occur during a live performance, where the artist's hiccups become a source of both humor and humility. The refrain, *"Every time I try to spit, I get a little hiccup, but that don't stop the beat, I just gotta pick it up!"* encapsulates the essence of turning a flaw into a strength. The relatability lies in the acknowledgment that everyone has faced similar moments of embarrassment and has had to find a way to push through.

Building Empathy Through Humor

Hiccups can also serve as a vehicle for humor in storytelling. When artists share their hiccup experiences, they invite the audience to laugh along with them. This laughter fosters a sense of community, as it highlights our shared human follies. For example, in a track titled *"Hiccups and Heartbreaks"*, the artist recounts a date gone wrong due to uncontrollable hiccups. The humorous depiction of the situation allows listeners to empathize with the artist's plight, making them feel as if they are part of the story.

The use of humor in hiccup narratives can be analyzed through the lens of **Benign Violation Theory**, which posits that humor arises when something is simultaneously perceived as a violation of social norms and benign. Hiccups, while often seen as socially awkward, are harmless and can be laughed at, making them a perfect subject for relatable storytelling.

Creating Relatable Characters

Incorporating hiccups into narratives also allows artists to create relatable characters within their songs. These characters can embody traits that listeners recognize in themselves or in people they know. For instance, an artist might describe a character who struggles with anxiety and, as a result, experiences hiccups in high-pressure situations. This narrative not only highlights the character's vulnerabilities but also encourages listeners to reflect on their own experiences with anxiety and stress.

$$\text{Relatability} = \frac{\text{Shared Experiences} + \text{Emotional Resonance}}{\text{Authenticity}} \qquad (47)$$

This equation suggests that relatability increases when shared experiences and emotional resonance are combined with authenticity. Hiccup narratives can enhance this equation by providing a unique lens through which listeners can view their own lives.

Examples of Hiccup Narratives in Hip Hop

Several hip hop artists have successfully utilized hiccup narratives to create relatable content. For example, in *"Stutter and Stumble"*, the artist recounts a series of life events that led to a moment of self-discovery, punctuated by his frequent hiccups. The lyrics, *"Stutter through the struggle, but I never lose the hustle,"* encapsulate the essence of resilience in the face of adversity.

Another example is *"Hiccups in the City"*, where the artist uses the metaphor of hiccups to describe the unpredictable nature of urban life. The narrative explores themes of survival, adaptability, and the importance of finding humor in chaotic situations, making it relatable to anyone who has navigated the complexities of city living.

Conclusion

In conclusion, relatability through hiccup narratives offers a powerful tool for hip hop artists to connect with their audience. By embracing imperfections and sharing personal stories, artists can foster a sense of community and understanding among listeners. Hiccups, whether they manifest as physical interruptions or metaphorical obstacles, serve as a reminder that we all share similar struggles. As artists continue to explore this theme, they not only enrich their own narratives but also create a space where listeners feel seen, heard, and understood.

Collaborating with Hiccup-Prone Artists

Finding Synergy with Other Vocal Quirks

In the vibrant world of hip hop, the uniqueness of each artist's voice can be a powerful tool for collaboration. When you embrace your own vocal quirks, such as hiccups, stutters, or even unique tonal qualities, you open the door to finding synergy with other artists who possess their own distinctive vocal traits. This section explores how to identify and collaborate with fellow artists who share or complement your vocal idiosyncrasies, creating a rich tapestry of sound that resonates with authenticity and creativity.

Understanding Vocal Quirks

Vocal quirks can be defined as the unique characteristics of a person's voice that set them apart from others. These can include:

- **Hiccups:** Sudden, involuntary contractions of the diaphragm, producing a distinctive sound.

- **Stutters:** Disruptions in the flow of speech, often characterized by repetitions or prolonged sounds.

- **Vocal Fry:** A low, creaky sound produced by a relaxed vocal fold, often used for stylistic effect.

- **Pitch Variations:** Unusual fluctuations in pitch that can add emotional depth or humor.

Each of these quirks can serve as an artistic signature, allowing artists to express their individuality while also providing opportunities for collaboration.

Theoretical Framework for Collaboration

To effectively collaborate with other artists who have vocal quirks, it's essential to understand the theoretical underpinnings of sound and rhythm. One useful framework is the concept of **synergy**, defined as the interaction of elements that produce a total effect greater than the sum of the individual elements. In mathematical terms, this can be represented as:

$$S = A + B + C + \ldots + n$$

where S is the synergistic outcome, and $A, B, C, \ldots n$ are the individual contributions of each artist's vocal quirk.

This formula highlights how different vocal styles can complement one another, leading to a richer auditory experience. For example, a hiccup can create a rhythmic pause that enhances the flow of a stutter, while vocal fry can provide a contrasting texture that adds depth to a melody.

Identifying Compatible Vocal Quirks

Finding synergy begins with identifying artists who possess vocal quirks that can either complement or contrast with your own. Here are some strategies to consider:

1. **Listen Actively:** Pay attention to local and online artists who showcase their unique vocal styles. Platforms like SoundCloud and Bandcamp can be treasure troves for discovering emerging talents.

2. **Attend Open Mics:** Engaging with live performances allows you to experience artists' vocal quirks in real-time. This setting also provides an opportunity to network and explore potential collaborations.

3. **Collaborative Workshops:** Participate in workshops or jam sessions focused on improvisation. This environment encourages experimentation with different vocal styles, allowing you to identify synergies organically.

Case Studies

To illustrate the concept of finding synergy with other vocal quirks, we can examine a few notable collaborations in the hip hop genre:

- **Chance the Rapper and Lil Wayne:** In their collaboration on "No Problem," Chance's playful hiccup-like delivery complements Lil Wayne's rapid-fire staccato flow. The interplay of their vocal styles creates a dynamic listening experience that showcases both artists' strengths.

- **Eminem and Dido:** In "Stan," Eminem's rhythmic stuttering and Dido's hauntingly smooth vocals create a haunting contrast. This synergy enhances the emotional weight of the narrative, illustrating how vocal quirks can work together to tell a powerful story.

- **Busta Rhymes and Spliff Star:** Their collaborations often feature Busta's rapid-fire delivery and Spliff's unique vocal inflections. The combination of their vocal quirks results in an energetic and engaging performance that captivates audiences.

Practical Exercises for Synergy

To cultivate synergy with other artists, consider the following exercises:

1. **Vocal Jam Sessions:** Organize informal sessions with fellow artists to explore each other's vocal quirks. Focus on improvisation and experimentation, allowing your unique sounds to blend and evolve.

2. **Create a Hiccup Challenge:** Challenge fellow artists to incorporate hiccups into their verses. This playful exercise can lead to unexpected and creative outcomes, fostering collaboration and camaraderie.

3. **Record and Analyze:** Collaborate on a track and record the session. Analyze the playback to identify moments where your vocal quirks synergize. Use this feedback to refine your collaborative approach.

Conclusion

Finding synergy with other vocal quirks is an enriching journey that can elevate your hip hop artistry. By embracing your own unique vocal characteristics and seeking out like-minded artists, you can create a collaborative environment that celebrates individuality while producing a collective sound that resonates with authenticity. Remember, the beauty of hip hop lies in its diversity, and your hiccups, stutters, and quirks are not just obstacles but powerful tools for creative expression. Embrace them, and watch as they transform your music into something truly extraordinary.

Harnessing the Unique Sound of Hiccup Collaborations

Collaborating with other artists can be a transformative experience, especially when both parties embrace the quirks of their vocal styles. In this section, we will explore how to harness the unique sound of hiccup collaborations, turning what might be perceived as a flaw into a defining characteristic of your music.

Understanding the Hiccup Sound

Hiccups are involuntary contractions of the diaphragm, often producing a distinctive sound that can be rhythmic and catchy. This sound can be likened to a staccato note in music, where the abruptness can add a unique texture to a track. To fully utilize this sound in collaborations, it is essential to understand its acoustic properties.

The hiccup can be characterized by the following parameters:

$$f = \frac{1}{T} \qquad (48)$$

where f is the frequency of the hiccup sound, and T is the duration of the hiccup in seconds. This relationship shows how the timing of hiccups can influence the rhythm and flow of a song.

Finding Synergy with Other Vocal Quirks

When collaborating with other artists, it is crucial to find synergy between your hiccup sounds and their unique vocal characteristics. For instance, if you are working with a vocalist who has a raspy voice, the contrast between their sound and your hiccup can create an engaging auditory experience.

Consider the collaboration between artists like *Dizzee Rascal* and *Arctic Monkeys*, where the combination of rap and rock elements led to a fresh sound. Similarly, incorporating hiccups into a duet or group performance can enhance the overall texture of the music.

To achieve this synergy, try the following techniques:

- **Layering Sounds:** Record multiple tracks of hiccups and blend them with the collaborator's vocals. Experiment with different effects, such as reverb and delay, to create a rich soundscape.

- **Call and Response:** Create a call-and-response pattern where one artist delivers a line, and the other responds with a hiccup. This technique can add a playful and engaging element to the performance.

COLLABORATING WITH HICCUP-PRONE ARTISTS

- **Complementary Rhythms:** Analyze the rhythm patterns of your collaborator's delivery and find ways to incorporate hiccups that complement their flow. This can involve syncing your hiccups with specific beats or syllables in their lyrics.

Harnessing the Unique Sound in Production

In the studio, the production process is where the magic happens. To effectively harness the unique sound of hiccup collaborations, consider the following production techniques:

- **Sampling Hiccups:** Use software to sample the hiccup sounds and manipulate them. Adjust the pitch, speed, and effects to create unique sounds that can serve as hooks or background elements in your track.

- **Creating Hiccup Beats:** Develop drum patterns that mimic the rhythm of hiccups. For example, you can use a kick drum to represent the initial contraction and a snare for the release, creating a hiccup-inspired beat.

- **Dynamic Mixing:** Pay attention to the levels of the hiccup sounds in relation to other elements in the mix. Ensure that they are prominent enough to be recognized but not overpowering. This balance is key to maintaining the integrity of the collaboration.

Examples of Successful Hiccup Collaborations

To further illustrate the power of hiccup collaborations, let's look at a few examples from the hip hop world where artists have successfully integrated unique vocal quirks into their music:

- **Lil Wayne and Nicki Minaj:** In their track "Truffle Butter," both artists play with vocal inflections, including hiccup-like sounds, to create a dynamic interplay that enhances the lyrical flow.

- **Kendrick Lamar and SZA:** Their collaboration on "All the Stars" features a rhythmic pattern that includes hiccup-like pauses, adding depth and emotion to the storytelling aspect of the song.

- **Missy Elliott and Pharrell Williams:** In "Get Ur Freak On," Missy's playful use of hiccup sounds complements Pharrell's production, creating an infectious groove that resonates with listeners.

Conclusion

Harnessing the unique sound of hiccup collaborations requires an open mind and a willingness to experiment. By understanding the acoustic properties of hiccups, finding synergy with other artists, and employing creative production techniques, you can transform what may seem like a limitation into a powerful tool for artistic expression. Embrace the hiccups, and let them guide you to new and exciting musical landscapes. Remember, the beauty of hip hop lies in its imperfections, and hiccups can add a layer of authenticity that resonates with audiences.

Supporting and Inspiring Fellow Hiccup-Prone Artists

In the vibrant world of hip hop, collaboration and support among artists can create a powerful community that thrives on creativity and shared experiences. For those who find themselves hiccup-prone, fostering a supportive environment can transform the challenges of hiccups into a source of inspiration and innovation. This section explores the importance of supporting fellow artists, the benefits of collaboration, and practical strategies for creating an inclusive space for hiccup-prone musicians.

Finding Synergy with Other Vocal Quirks

Just as each hiccup is unique, so too is each artist's vocal style. Recognizing and embracing these differences can lead to exciting collaborations that highlight the strengths of each individual. For instance, consider the partnership between two artists, one with a stuttering delivery and another with a hiccup-infused flow. By combining their distinctive styles, they can create a rhythm that is both captivating and original.

Mathematically, we can represent the synergy of their collaboration as follows:

$$C = A + B + (A \cdot B) \tag{49}$$

Where:

- C is the collaborative output,
- A is the unique style of the first artist,
- B is the unique style of the second artist,
- $A \cdot B$ represents the interaction and enhancement of both styles.

This equation illustrates that the sum of their individual contributions, combined with the synergy of their collaboration, leads to a richer and more dynamic artistic output.

Harnessing the Unique Sound of Hiccup Collaborations

Hiccup-prone artists can harness their unique vocal characteristics to create a signature sound that resonates with audiences. For example, an artist might incorporate hiccup rhythms into their verses, using them as a form of punctuation or emphasis. This can create a distinctive sonic identity that sets them apart in the crowded hip hop landscape.

A notable example is the collaboration between artists who intentionally incorporate hiccup-like sounds into their hooks. This technique not only showcases their individual quirks but also adds a playful element to their music. By embracing these vocal idiosyncrasies, artists can inspire each other to push the boundaries of traditional hip hop.

Supporting and Inspiring Fellow Hiccup-Prone Artists

Creating a supportive network for hiccup-prone artists involves several key strategies:

1. **Encouragement and Validation:** Artists should actively encourage each other to embrace their hiccups as a natural part of their creative expression. Sharing personal stories of overcoming challenges can foster a sense of camaraderie and inspire others to do the same. For instance, an artist who has successfully incorporated hiccups into their flow can share their journey through social media or workshops, demonstrating that imperfections can lead to unique artistry.

2. **Collaborative Projects:** Organizing collaborative projects, such as mixtapes or performances, can provide hiccup-prone artists with opportunities to showcase their talents together. These projects can highlight the diversity of styles and encourage experimentation. For example, a collective of hiccup-prone artists might release a compilation album, each contributing tracks that feature their unique vocal quirks, ultimately creating a cohesive yet varied listening experience.

3. **Workshops and Masterclasses:** Hosting workshops focused on embracing vocal quirks can be a great way to build community. These sessions can

include exercises on how to incorporate hiccups into lyrical delivery, rhythm, and flow. Additionally, inviting experienced artists to share their techniques can inspire newcomers to explore their own hiccup styles.

4. **Online Platforms and Social Media:** Utilizing online platforms to share music, tips, and experiences can connect hiccup-prone artists globally. Creating hashtags like #HiccupHipHop or #HiccupArtists can help build a community where artists share their work and support one another.

5. **Mentorship Programs:** Establishing mentorship programs where experienced artists guide newcomers can foster growth and confidence. Mentors can provide constructive feedback, share resources, and offer advice on how to navigate the unique challenges of being a hiccup-prone artist.

Conclusion

Supporting and inspiring fellow hiccup-prone artists is essential for cultivating a thriving hip hop community. By embracing the uniqueness of each artist's voice and fostering collaboration, we can transform the challenges of hiccups into a source of strength and creativity. As we continue to share our experiences and support one another, we pave the way for a more inclusive and innovative future in hip hop, where every hiccup is celebrated as part of the art.

In this journey, remember: every hiccup is a beat waiting to be expressed. Let's turn those hiccups into anthems of creativity and connection.

Developing Your Unique Hiccup Style

Embracing and Refining Your Hiccup Sound

Experimenting with Different Hiccup Frequencies and Intensities

In the world of hip hop, rhythm is king, and the ability to innovate within that rhythm can lead to the creation of truly unique music. One of the most unconventional yet fascinating methods of experimentation is to explore the different frequencies and intensities of hiccups in your vocal delivery. This section delves into the theory behind hiccup frequencies, the problems associated with their integration into hip hop, and practical examples to inspire your creative process.

Understanding Hiccup Frequencies

Hiccups occur due to involuntary contractions of the diaphragm, followed by a sudden closure of the vocal cords, which produces the characteristic sound. The frequency of hiccups can be understood as the rate at which these contractions occur. Mathematically, frequency (f) is defined as the number of occurrences of a repeating event per unit time, typically measured in hertz (Hz):

$$f = \frac{n}{t} \tag{50}$$

where n is the number of hiccups and t is the time in seconds. For instance, if an artist hiccups 10 times in 5 seconds, the frequency of hiccups would be:

$$f = \frac{10}{5} = 2\,\text{Hz} \tag{51}$$

In hip hop, varying the frequency of hiccups can create distinct rhythmic patterns that enhance the overall flow of the track. For example, a high-frequency hiccup pattern (e.g., 4 Hz) can add a sense of urgency and excitement, while a lower frequency (e.g., 1 Hz) can introduce a laid-back, relaxed vibe.

Intensity of Hiccups

Intensity refers to the strength or force of the hiccup sound. This can be manipulated through vocal techniques, breath control, and even microphone placement during recording. The intensity of a hiccup can be measured in decibels (dB), where a higher dB level indicates a louder sound. The relationship between sound intensity and pressure is given by:

$$L = 10 \log_{10}\left(\frac{I}{I_0}\right) \quad (52)$$

where L is the sound level in decibels, I is the intensity of the sound, and I_0 is the reference intensity, typically 10^{-12} W/m^2.

In hip hop, varying the intensity of hiccups can evoke different emotional responses. A soft, subtle hiccup can create a sense of intimacy or vulnerability, while a loud, forceful hiccup can convey power and confidence. Consider how you can play with these dynamics in your tracks.

Challenges in Integrating Hiccups

While experimenting with hiccup frequencies and intensities can lead to innovative sounds, there are challenges to consider:

- **Consistency:** Maintaining a consistent frequency and intensity can be difficult, especially when performing live. Artists must practice to ensure that their hiccup delivery aligns with the beat and overall flow of the song.

- **Audience Perception:** Not all listeners may appreciate the use of hiccups in hip hop. It's essential to gauge your audience's reaction and adjust accordingly. Some may find hiccups distracting, while others may embrace them as a unique feature of your style.

- **Recording Quality:** Capturing the nuanced frequencies and intensities of hiccups can be challenging in a studio setting. Proper microphone techniques and sound engineering are crucial to ensure that hiccups are heard clearly without distortion.

Practical Examples

To illustrate the application of hiccup frequencies and intensities, let's examine a few artists known for their innovative use of vocal techniques:

- **Busta Rhymes:** Renowned for his rapid-fire delivery, Busta often incorporates hiccup-like sounds at high frequencies to enhance his verses. His track "Break Ya Neck" showcases how a rapid hiccup pattern can create a thrilling and energizing effect.

- **Lil Wayne:** Known for his unique vocal style, Wayne often uses hiccups at varying intensities to add character to his lyrics. In "A Milli," he integrates softer hiccups to create a sense of intimacy amidst powerful lyrics.

- **Missy Elliott:** Missy is a pioneer in using vocal hiccups creatively. In "Work It," she employs hiccup sounds at different frequencies to complement the beat, showcasing how these sounds can be rhythmically engaging and memorable.

Conclusion

Experimenting with different hiccup frequencies and intensities can transform your hip hop tracks into something truly original. By understanding the science behind hiccups and their potential impact on your music, you can push the boundaries of traditional hip hop. Embrace the quirks, play with the sounds, and let your creativity flow—hiccups and all. As you refine your unique style, remember that the beauty of hip hop lies in its ability to evolve and innovate, just like the art of hiccuping itself.

Incorporating Hiccup-Like Vocal Effects

In the world of hip hop, vocal delivery is an essential component that can elevate a track from ordinary to extraordinary. One innovative approach to achieving a unique sound is through the use of hiccup-like vocal effects. These effects can add texture, rhythm, and character to your music, making it stand out in a crowded genre. In this section, we will explore the theory behind incorporating these effects, the challenges you may face, and practical examples to inspire your creativity.

Understanding Hiccup-Like Vocal Effects

Hiccups are involuntary contractions of the diaphragm, often resulting in a distinctive sound. In a musical context, this sound can be emulated or exaggerated to create hiccup-like vocal effects. These effects can serve multiple purposes, such as adding humor, creating tension, or enhancing the rhythmic flow of a track. The primary theoretical foundation for these effects lies in the principles of sound modulation and rhythm.

The sound of a hiccup can be broken down into its fundamental frequency and harmonics. The fundamental frequency (f_0) can be defined as:

$$f_0 = \frac{1}{T} \tag{53}$$

where T is the period of the sound wave. The harmonics can be represented as integer multiples of the fundamental frequency:

$$f_n = n \cdot f_0 \quad \text{for } n = 1, 2, 3, \ldots \tag{54}$$

By understanding these principles, you can manipulate your vocal delivery to mimic the irregularities and spontaneity of hiccups.

Techniques for Incorporating Hiccup-Like Effects

There are several techniques to effectively incorporate hiccup-like vocal effects into your hip hop tracks:

- **Vocal Sampling:** Record yourself or other artists making hiccup sounds. These samples can then be manipulated using digital audio workstations (DAWs) to create unique vocal textures. Experiment with pitch shifting, time-stretching, and layering to enhance the effect.

- **Vocal Modulation:** Use pitch modulation and vocal fry techniques to create a hiccup-like sound. By varying the pitch and intensity of your voice, you can replicate the erratic nature of hiccups. This can be achieved through vocal exercises that focus on breath control and diaphragm strength.

- **Rhythmic Insertion:** Incorporate hiccup-like sounds into your flow by strategically placing them within your verses. For instance, you can insert a hiccup sound at the end of a line or between words to create an unexpected pause that adds character to your delivery.

- **Effects Processing:** Utilize audio effects such as distortion, reverb, and delay to enhance the hiccup-like quality of your vocals. By processing your voice through these effects, you can create a more pronounced and engaging sound.

Challenges and Solutions

While incorporating hiccup-like vocal effects can be rewarding, it also presents certain challenges:

- **Maintaining Clarity:** One of the primary challenges is ensuring that the hiccup effects do not obscure the clarity of your lyrics. To mitigate this, practice your delivery to ensure that the hiccup sounds blend seamlessly with your flow. Consider using EQ to carve out space in the mix for both your vocals and the hiccup effects.

- **Avoiding Overuse:** Overusing hiccup effects can lead to a cluttered sound. To avoid this, use these effects sparingly and purposefully. Consider reserving hiccup sounds for specific moments in your track, such as transitions or climactic points, to maximize their impact.

- **Finding Your Voice:** It can be challenging to find the right balance between your natural vocal style and the hiccup-like effects. Experiment with different techniques and approaches until you discover a sound that feels authentic to you.

Examples of Hiccup-Like Vocal Effects in Hip Hop

To inspire your creativity, here are a few examples of hip hop artists who have successfully incorporated hiccup-like vocal effects into their music:

- **Lil Wayne:** Known for his playful vocal delivery, Lil Wayne often uses hiccup-like sounds to punctuate his verses. His unique flow and rhythmic insertion of these sounds create a dynamic listening experience.

- **Busta Rhymes:** Busta is celebrated for his rapid-fire delivery and playful vocal effects. His ability to weave hiccup-like sounds into his verses adds an element of surprise and keeps listeners engaged.

- **Missy Elliott:** Missy's innovative approach to vocal effects includes the use of hiccup-like sounds to enhance her storytelling. By incorporating these effects, she adds depth and character to her narratives.

Conclusion

Incorporating hiccup-like vocal effects into your hip hop tracks can provide a fresh and engaging sound that sets you apart from the crowd. By understanding the theory behind these effects, employing various techniques, and learning from successful artists, you can develop your unique style that embraces the beauty of imperfections. Remember, the key to success lies in experimentation and finding what resonates with your artistic vision. So, let your creativity flow, and don't be afraid to embrace the hiccups along the way!

Finding Your Signature Hiccup Style

Finding your unique hiccup style is akin to discovering your voice in the vast world of hip hop. This process involves experimenting with various hiccup frequencies, intensities, and vocal effects to create a sound that is distinctly yours. In this section, we will explore the intricacies of developing your signature hiccup style, the importance of personal expression, and how to incorporate these elements into your music.

Experimenting with Different Hiccup Frequencies and Intensities

The first step in defining your signature hiccup style is to experiment with the frequency and intensity of your hiccups. Hiccups can vary significantly in their sound, from soft and subtle to loud and jarring.

$$f_h = \frac{1}{T} \tag{55}$$

where f_h is the frequency of hiccups and T is the duration between each hiccup. By manipulating the timing and intensity of your hiccups, you can create unique rhythmic patterns that enhance your flow.

For example, consider the difference between a rapid succession of soft hiccups versus a single, powerful hiccup. The former can create a playful, bouncy rhythm, while the latter may add a dramatic pause that emphasizes a particular lyric or beat.

Incorporating Hiccup-Like Vocal Effects

In addition to natural hiccups, you can enhance your signature style by incorporating hiccup-like vocal effects. This could include vocal techniques such as:

- **Vocal Fry:** A low, creaky sound that can mimic the texture of a hiccup.

- **Glottal Stops:** Quick closures of the vocal cords that can create a hiccup-like interruption in your delivery.

EMBRACING AND REFINING YOUR HICCUP SOUND

- **Pitch Variation:** Altering your pitch during a hiccup to add emotional depth or comedic effect.

These techniques can be combined with your natural hiccup sounds to create a rich, textured vocal style. For instance, an artist might use a vocal fry during a hiccup to add a gritty, raw quality to their delivery, making the hiccups feel more integrated into their overall sound.

Finding Your Signature Hiccup Style

To truly find your signature hiccup style, it is essential to embrace the process of trial and error. Here are some steps to guide you:

1. **Record Yourself:** Start by recording various hiccup sounds and vocal techniques. Play around with different styles, speeds, and intensities. Listen back to identify what resonates with you.

2. **Analyze Your Influences:** Listen to artists known for their unique vocal styles. Analyze how they incorporate hiccups and other vocal quirks into their music. Consider how you can adapt these techniques to fit your artistic vision.

3. **Create a Hiccup Palette:** Develop a collection of your favorite hiccup sounds and techniques. This palette will serve as a reference for your writing and recording sessions, helping you to maintain consistency in your style.

4. **Collaborate:** Work with other artists who have a unique approach to their vocal delivery. Collaborations can inspire new ideas and push you to explore different aspects of your hiccup style.

Examples of Signature Hiccup Styles

Many artists have successfully integrated hiccups into their music, creating signature styles that set them apart. For instance:

- **Busta Rhymes:** Known for his rapid-fire delivery, Busta often incorporates abrupt pauses and hiccup-like sounds that enhance his rhythmic flow.

- **Lil Wayne:** His distinctive vocal style includes playful hiccups that add a layer of personality to his tracks, making his delivery feel more conversational.

- **Missy Elliott:** She often uses hiccup-like vocal effects to create a playful and engaging sound, making her music memorable and infectious.

These artists demonstrate how hiccups can be an integral part of a unique vocal identity. By studying their techniques and experimenting with your own, you can develop a signature hiccup style that reflects your personality and artistic vision.

Conclusion

Finding your signature hiccup style is a journey of self-discovery and experimentation. By exploring different frequencies, intensities, and vocal effects, you can create a sound that is uniquely yours. Embrace the quirks and imperfections that come with hiccups, and let them inspire your creativity. Remember, the beauty of hip hop lies in its diversity and authenticity, so let your hiccups be a defining aspect of your musical identity.

Using Hiccups as a Creative Constraint

Pushing Boundaries with Hiccup-Infused Hip Hop

In the vibrant landscape of hip hop, pushing boundaries is not just encouraged; it's essential. Hiccup-infused hip hop offers a unique lens through which to explore creativity, rhythm, and expression. This section delves into how artists can leverage the unpredictable nature of hiccups to break through conventional barriers and create innovative sounds.

The Concept of Creative Constraints

Creative constraints can often lead to unexpected breakthroughs. When artists embrace the idea of incorporating hiccups—both literal and metaphorical—into their music, they open themselves up to new possibilities. The hiccup, typically seen as an interruption, can be reframed as a rhythmic element that adds texture and depth to a track.

Consider the equation for rhythm in music, which can be expressed as:

$$R = B + V + L \tag{56}$$

Where:

- R = Rhythm

USING HICCUPS AS A CREATIVE CONSTRAINT

- B = Beat
- V = Vocal delivery
- L = Lyrics

By introducing hiccups into the vocal delivery V, artists can create a new dimension of rhythm that challenges traditional expectations. This can lead to a more dynamic and engaging listening experience.

Examples of Hiccup-Infused Innovation

One of the most notable examples of boundary-pushing in hip hop is the work of artists like *MF DOOM* and *Danny Brown*. Both artists have utilized unconventional vocal techniques, including stutters and hiccup-like interruptions, to create distinct styles that defy the norm.

For instance, in MF DOOM's track "Rapp Snitch Knishes," the irregularities in his flow, punctuated by unexpected pauses and hiccup-like inflections, create a unique listening experience. This technique not only emphasizes the lyrical content but also contributes to the overall groove of the song. The deliberate use of hiccups in his delivery showcases how breaking free from traditional flow can enhance the narrative and emotional impact of the music.

Theoretical Implications of Hiccups in Hip Hop

From a theoretical standpoint, incorporating hiccups can be analyzed through the lens of *musical dissonance* and *resolution*. Dissonance occurs when sounds clash, creating tension, while resolution occurs when these tensions are resolved. Hiccups can serve as a form of dissonance in hip hop, introducing unexpected elements that challenge the listener's expectations.

This can be illustrated mathematically by considering the dissonance D created by hiccups in a musical phrase:

$$D = \sum_{i=1}^{n}(F_i - T_i) \tag{57}$$

Where:

- D = Dissonance
- F_i = Frequency of hiccup-infused notes

- T_i = Target frequency of the expected rhythm

As artists experiment with different frequencies and intensities of hiccups, they can manipulate the level of dissonance, leading to a richer and more complex musical texture.

Challenges and Solutions

While pushing boundaries with hiccup-infused hip hop offers exciting opportunities, it also presents challenges. Artists may struggle with balancing the unpredictability of hiccups with the need for coherence in their tracks. The key lies in finding the right moments to incorporate hiccups without overwhelming the listener.

One effective strategy is to use hiccups as transitional elements. For example, an artist might introduce a hiccup during a bridge or a breakdown, allowing for a moment of surprise that reinvigorates the listener's attention. This technique not only maintains the flow of the track but also enhances the overall narrative arc.

Conclusion: Embracing the Hiccup Revolution

Pushing boundaries with hiccup-infused hip hop is not merely about incorporating a quirky vocal technique; it's about redefining what hip hop can be. By embracing the unpredictable nature of hiccups, artists can create innovative sounds that challenge conventions and resonate with audiences on a deeper level. As we continue to explore the intersection of hip hop and hiccups, we invite you to experiment, innovate, and push your own creative boundaries.

In the words of *Kendrick Lamar*, "We gon' be alright," especially when we allow ourselves to embrace the hiccups along the way.

Overcoming Challenges and Limitations with Hiccups

In the world of Hip Hop, hiccups can be perceived as both a challenge and an opportunity. Just as a great artist learns to navigate the complexities of their craft, embracing the hiccups in your creative process can lead to unexpected breakthroughs. This section explores how to transform limitations posed by hiccups into powerful tools for artistic expression.

Understanding the Challenge

Hiccups, while often seen as a nuisance, can disrupt the flow of creativity and performance. They may lead to moments of hesitation or awkwardness, especially

USING HICCUPS AS A CREATIVE CONSTRAINT

in the fast-paced environment of Hip Hop. The challenge lies in the way these interruptions can affect rhythm, delivery, and overall performance.

Consider the scenario of a freestyle battle. A sudden hiccup can break your flow, causing you to lose your rhythm and potentially your confidence. However, it's essential to recognize that these moments can also serve as catalysts for creativity. The key is to reframe your mindset regarding these interruptions.

Reframing Limitations

When faced with hiccups, it's crucial to shift your perspective from viewing them as hindrances to seeing them as opportunities for innovation. This can be achieved through several strategies:

- **Acceptance:** Acknowledge that hiccups are a natural part of the creative process. Accepting their presence allows you to focus on what you can control—your response to them.

- **Adaptation:** Develop the ability to adapt your flow and delivery in response to hiccups. This flexibility can enhance your performance, making it more dynamic and engaging.

- **Creativity:** Use hiccups as a springboard for creativity. Incorporate them into your lyrics or beats, turning what could be a distraction into a unique element of your style.

Practical Techniques for Overcoming Hiccups

To effectively overcome the challenges posed by hiccups, consider implementing the following practical techniques:

1. Breathing Techniques Breathing exercises can be invaluable in managing hiccups. Controlled breathing helps to calm the nervous system and can reduce the frequency of hiccups during performance.

For instance, try the following technique:

1. Inhale deeply through your nose for a count of four.

2. Hold your breath for a count of four.

3. Exhale slowly through your mouth for a count of six.

Repeat this cycle several times before performing to help mitigate the risk of hiccups.

2. Incorporating Hiccups into Your Flow Instead of trying to suppress hiccups, incorporate them into your performance. For example, consider the following technique:

$$\text{New Flow} = \text{Original Flow} + \text{Hiccup Interruption} \qquad (58)$$

This equation illustrates how hiccups can be added into your existing flow, creating a unique rhythm that enhances your delivery.

3. Practice and Rehearsal Regular practice is essential for mastering your flow. During rehearsals, intentionally introduce hiccups into your performance to become comfortable with navigating interruptions. This practice can desensitize you to the anxiety that may accompany unexpected hiccups during live performances.

Examples of Successful Adaptation

Many successful Hip Hop artists have turned their challenges into triumphs by embracing the unpredictable nature of their craft. For instance, consider the case of **Eminem**, who has often spoken about his struggles with anxiety and how it manifests during performances. Instead of allowing these challenges to hinder his artistry, he channels them into his lyrics, creating a relatable narrative that resonates with fans.

Similarly, **Busta Rhymes** is known for his rapid-fire delivery, which includes moments of intentional pauses that mimic hiccups. This technique not only showcases his skill but also adds an engaging element to his performances, demonstrating how hiccups can enhance rather than detract from the overall experience.

Conclusion

In conclusion, overcoming the challenges and limitations posed by hiccups requires a shift in mindset and the adoption of practical strategies. By embracing hiccups as part of your creative journey, you can transform potential setbacks into defining moments of your artistry. Remember, every hiccup can lead to a new rhythm, a fresh lyric, or an unforgettable performance. Embrace the unpredictability, and let your hiccups become a hallmark of your unique Hip Hop style.

Transforming Hiccups into a Defining Aspect of Your Music

In the world of hip hop, the beauty often lies in the unexpected. Just as a hiccup disrupts a conversation, it can also disrupt the flow of a track, creating a unique and

USING HICCUPS AS A CREATIVE CONSTRAINT

memorable sound. This section explores how to embrace and refine the hiccup as a defining aspect of your music, transforming what might be perceived as a flaw into a hallmark of originality and creativity.

Pushing Boundaries with Hiccup-Infused Hip Hop

The first step in transforming hiccups into a defining aspect of your music is to push the boundaries of traditional hip hop. Consider the following theoretical framework:

$$H = f(B, C, I) \tag{59}$$

Where:

- H = Hiccup-infused hip hop
- B = Boundary pushing in music
- C = Creativity and innovation
- I = Incorporation of hiccup elements

This equation emphasizes that the integration of hiccup elements into your tracks can lead to innovative and boundary-pushing music. To effectively utilize hiccups, you can experiment with various placements within your verses, hooks, and bridges. For instance, consider the work of artists like **Danny Brown**, whose distinctive vocal style often incorporates unexpected pauses and breaks, reminiscent of hiccups.

Overcoming Challenges and Limitations with Hiccups

While embracing hiccups can lead to unique sounds, it may also present challenges. You might encounter a few common problems, such as:

- **Consistency:** Maintaining a coherent flow while incorporating hiccups can be difficult.
- **Audience Reception:** Listeners may initially be taken aback by the unconventional use of hiccups.
- **Self-Doubt:** As an artist, you may question whether your hiccup-inspired style is valid.

To overcome these challenges, consider the following strategies:

1. **Practice and Experimentation:** Regularly practice incorporating hiccups into your writing and performance. Use freestyle sessions to explore different ways of integrating these interruptions into your flow.

2. **Feedback Loops:** Share your music with trusted peers and mentors. Constructive feedback can help you refine your sound and build confidence in your unique style.

3. **Audience Engagement:** Use social media and live performances to gauge audience reactions. Engaging with your listeners can provide insights into how they perceive your hiccup-infused style.

Transforming Hiccups into a Defining Aspect of Your Music

To truly transform hiccups into a defining aspect of your music, you must embrace the concept of *creative constraints*. By intentionally limiting certain elements, you can foster innovation. For example, you could limit your lyrical structure to only use hiccup-like interruptions or pauses. This method can lead to unexpected lyrical patterns and rhythms.

Consider the following example:

> "I'm spitting bars, but wait—hiccup—let me catch my breath. Life's a test, hiccup—can you feel the stress?"

In this example, the hiccup serves as both a rhythmic and thematic element, adding depth to the narrative while creating a memorable listening experience.

Finding Your Signature Hiccup Style

To solidify hiccups as a hallmark of your music, strive to develop a signature style. This process involves:

1. **Identifying Your Unique Sound:** Experiment with different frequencies and intensities of hiccups. Are they soft and subtle, or loud and jarring?

2. **Incorporating Vocal Effects:** Use vocal processing tools to manipulate your hiccups, creating a distinct sound that resonates with your artistic vision.

3. **Creating a Cohesive Brand:** Ensure that your hiccup style aligns with your overall artistic identity. This consistency will help audiences recognize and connect with your music.

Conclusion

By transforming hiccups into a defining aspect of your music, you not only embrace your imperfections but also create a unique sound that sets you apart in the hip hop landscape. As you push boundaries, overcome challenges, and refine your style, remember that your hiccups are not just interruptions; they are an integral part of your artistic expression.

In the words of **Kendrick Lamar**, "The best way to be yourself is to embrace your flaws." So, let your hiccups flow and watch as they transform your music into something truly extraordinary.

Hiccup-Inspired Performance Techniques

Engaging the Audience with Hiccup Gestures

Engaging an audience is a crucial aspect of any performance, especially in the world of Hip Hop where connection and energy are paramount. Hiccup gestures, or physical movements inspired by the spontaneous and unpredictable nature of hiccups, can serve as a unique tool for artists to captivate their audience. This section explores the theory behind using hiccup gestures, the potential problems artists might face, and practical examples of how to effectively incorporate these gestures into performances.

Theoretical Framework

The concept of engaging the audience through hiccup gestures can be rooted in several theories of performance and audience interaction. One such theory is the *Embodied Interaction Theory*, which posits that physical presence and movement significantly influence how audiences perceive and connect with performers. Hiccups, being involuntary and often humorous, can break the ice and create a sense of relatability between the artist and the audience.

$$\text{Engagement} = f(\text{Gestures, Audience Response}) \tag{60}$$

In this equation, engagement is a function of the gestures performed by the artist and the corresponding response from the audience. Hiccup gestures, characterized by their spontaneity and unpredictability, can elicit laughter, surprise, or even empathy, enhancing audience engagement.

Potential Problems

While incorporating hiccup gestures can be effective, there are challenges to consider:

- **Misinterpretation:** Hiccup gestures might be misunderstood by the audience. If not executed with clarity, these gestures can come off as awkward rather than endearing.

- **Overuse:** Relying too heavily on hiccup gestures may detract from the overall performance. Balance is key; gestures should complement the music, not overshadow it.

- **Audience Reception:** Different audiences have varying thresholds for humor and spontaneity. What works in one setting might not resonate in another, requiring adaptability from the artist.

Practical Examples

To effectively engage the audience with hiccup gestures, consider the following strategies:

- **Incorporating Hiccup Sounds:** Use hiccup sounds as part of your vocal delivery. For instance, during a pause in the beat, let out a playful hiccup. This can create a moment of surprise and laughter, drawing the audience's attention.

- **Physical Representation:** Use exaggerated movements to mimic the action of hiccuping. A sudden jerk of the body or a playful hand gesture can visually represent the hiccup, making it a part of the performance's choreography. For example, during a particularly intense lyrical section, lean back and then snap forward as if caught in a hiccup.

- **Audience Interaction:** Encourage the audience to mimic your hiccup gestures. This creates a shared experience and fosters a sense of community. For instance, during a call-and-response section, you can hiccup and then prompt the audience to respond with their own hiccup-like sounds or movements.

- **Playful Storytelling:** Use hiccup gestures as part of a narrative in your performance. Imagine telling a story about a funny incident where you hiccuped at an embarrassing moment. Use your body language to illustrate the story, making the hiccup gesture a pivotal part of the narrative.

Conclusion

Incorporating hiccup gestures into a performance is not just about humor; it's about building a bridge between the artist and the audience. By understanding the theoretical background, being aware of potential problems, and applying practical examples, artists can create memorable performances that resonate with their audience. Remember, the key is to embrace the unpredictability of hiccups, transforming them from mere involuntary actions into a powerful tool for connection and engagement.

Connecting through Hiccup Interaction

In the vibrant world of hip hop, performance is not merely about delivering lyrics; it's about creating a visceral connection with the audience. Hiccups—those unexpected, involuntary spasms—can serve as a unique tool for interaction, transforming a standard performance into an engaging experience. This section explores how to leverage hiccup interactions to foster a deeper bond with your audience, enhancing both the performance and the overall enjoyment of your music.

The Power of Audience Engagement

Audience engagement is a cornerstone of successful performances. When artists invite their audience into the experience, they create a shared moment that transcends the stage. Hiccups, often perceived as awkward or embarrassing, can be reframed as a playful interaction point. By embracing these moments, artists can cultivate a more authentic connection with their fans.

For instance, consider a live performance where the artist acknowledges a hiccup during a verse. Instead of glossing over it, they can pause, laugh, and even incorporate the hiccup into their flow. This spontaneous moment not only lightens the atmosphere but also humanizes the artist, making them relatable. The audience is likely to respond with laughter or cheers, creating a shared experience that enhances the performance.

Creating Interactive Moments

To effectively connect through hiccup interaction, artists can implement several strategies:

- **Call and Response:** Engage the audience by inviting them to mimic hiccup sounds or rhythms. For example, an artist can say, "On the count of three, let's all hiccup together!" This not only breaks the ice but also creates a memorable, participatory moment.

- **Hiccup Challenges:** Introduce a playful challenge where the audience must incorporate hiccup sounds into their responses. This could be during a chorus or a specific part of the song, fostering a sense of community as everyone participates.

- **Storytelling with Hiccups:** Use hiccups as a storytelling device. Share a humorous or relatable story about a time when hiccups interrupted a performance or a personal moment. This narrative approach invites the audience into the artist's world, making them feel more connected.

Theoretical Framework: Social Interaction Theory

To understand the effectiveness of hiccup interactions, we can draw upon Social Interaction Theory. This theory posits that social interactions are fundamental to human experience, shaping our identities and relationships. In the context of hip hop, these interactions can be amplified through hiccups, which serve as a catalyst for connection.

Mathematically, we can represent the interaction between the artist and audience as follows:

$$C = f(A, H) \qquad (61)$$

Where:

- C represents the level of connection,

- A represents audience engagement strategies (e.g., call and response, storytelling),

- H represents the incorporation of hiccups into the performance.

The equation suggests that the connection C increases as the artist employs various audience engagement strategies A while integrating hiccups H. This interaction creates a feedback loop, enhancing the overall performance experience.

Examples from Renowned Artists

Several hip hop artists have effectively utilized hiccup interactions in their performances:

HICCUP-INSPIRED PERFORMANCE TECHNIQUES 121

- **Chance the Rapper:** Known for his engaging stage presence, Chance often incorporates audience participation into his shows. During one performance, he experienced a hiccup mid-verse and playfully invited the crowd to join him in a "hiccup chorus," creating a moment of unity and laughter.
- **Lil Dicky:** In his comedic style, Lil Dicky often uses hiccups as a punchline. During a live performance of "Freaky Friday," he paused to hiccup intentionally, prompting the audience to laugh and cheer, thereby enhancing the comedic timing of his act.

Challenges and Considerations

While engaging with hiccup interactions can be beneficial, artists must also navigate potential challenges:

- **Timing and Flow:** Integrating hiccup interactions must not disrupt the flow of the performance. Artists should practice timing to ensure that these moments feel natural rather than forced.
- **Audience Reception:** Not all audiences may respond positively to hiccup interactions. Artists should gauge their audience's mood and be prepared to pivot if the engagement strategy does not resonate.

Conclusion

Connecting through hiccup interaction is a powerful method for hip hop artists to engage their audience, creating memorable and authentic experiences. By embracing the unexpected, artists can transform potential awkwardness into moments of joy and connection. As you develop your unique style, consider how hiccup interactions can enhance your performances, making each show a shared journey with your audience.

In the world of hip hop, where authenticity reigns supreme, hiccups can be your secret weapon for building connections that resonate long after the last beat drops.

Making Hiccups Part of Your Stage Persona

The stage is a canvas, and every artist paints their story with unique strokes. For hip hop artists, the incorporation of personal quirks, such as hiccups, can transform a performance into an unforgettable experience. Embracing your hiccups as part of your stage persona not only enhances your authenticity but also creates a memorable connection with your audience. This section explores how to effectively integrate hiccups into your performance style, turning potential distractions into engaging elements of your artistry.

Understanding the Impact of Hiccups on Performance

Hiccups, often seen as nuisances, can actually serve as a powerful tool in performance. They introduce an element of unpredictability that can captivate an audience's attention. The key lies in understanding how to harness this unpredictability to enhance your stage presence.

Consider the following theoretical framework for integrating hiccups into your performance:

$$P = \frac{C + E + R}{T} \qquad (62)$$

Where:

- P = Performance Impact
- C = Connection with the audience
- E = Energy of the performance
- R = Relatability of the artist
- T = Timing of hiccups

The equation suggests that the overall impact of your performance can be maximized by balancing your connection with the audience, the energy you bring, your relatability, and the timing of your hiccups.

Creating a Hiccup-Inspired Stage Routine

To make hiccups a signature part of your stage persona, consider the following strategies:

1. **Embrace the Unexpected:** Use hiccups as a cue to engage with your audience. For example, if you experience a hiccup during a rap, pause, smile, and acknowledge it. This creates a moment of shared humor and breaks the fourth wall.

HICCUP-INSPIRED PERFORMANCE TECHNIQUES

2. **Incorporate Hiccups into Choreography:** Develop dance moves or gestures that mimic the rhythm of hiccups. This can create a visual representation of your unique sound and add an extra layer of entertainment. Think of it as a dance that punctuates your lyrics with movement that reflects your vocal quirks.

3. **Use Hiccups as a Call and Response Tool:** Encourage your audience to mimic your hiccups during certain parts of your performance. This not only engages them but also reinforces the idea that hiccups are a fun and integral part of your artistic identity.

4. **Create a Hiccup-Themed Merchandise:** Consider designing t-shirts or accessories that playfully reference hiccups. This can serve as a conversation starter and help fans connect more deeply with your stage persona.

Turning Hiccups into Performance Highlights

The most memorable performances often include unexpected moments that resonate with the audience. Here are a few examples of how hiccups can be transformed into highlights:

- **Storytelling with Hiccups:** Use hiccups to punctuate key moments in your lyrics. For instance, if you're telling a story about overcoming challenges, a well-timed hiccup can emphasize the struggle and add an element of humor.

- **Interactive Freestyling:** During freestyle sessions, incorporate hiccups intentionally. This can lead to spontaneous and humorous rhymes that keep the audience engaged and entertained.

- **Collaborative Hiccup Moments:** If performing with other artists, coordinate hiccup moments to create a unique interplay. This can be a signature move that sets your performances apart, showcasing the chemistry between artists.

Audience Engagement and Connection

The relationship between performer and audience is vital in hip hop. By making hiccups a part of your stage persona, you foster a sense of relatability. Audiences appreciate vulnerability and authenticity, and embracing your hiccups can humanize you as an artist.

$$E = \frac{H + C + R}{A} \qquad (63)$$

Where:

- E = Audience Engagement
- H = Hiccups utilized in performance
- C = Connection established with the audience
- R = Relatability of the artist
- A = Audience size

This equation indicates that the level of audience engagement can be enhanced by effectively using hiccups, establishing a strong connection, and maintaining relatability, regardless of the audience size.

Conclusion

Incorporating hiccups into your stage persona is not just about embracing a physical quirk; it's about redefining how you engage with your audience and express your artistry. By turning hiccups into an integral part of your performance, you create a unique identity that resonates with fans and sets you apart in the hip hop landscape. Remember, the stage is your playground—make it a space where hiccups are celebrated, not hidden, and watch as your performances transform into unforgettable experiences.

By embracing the unexpected, you can turn every hiccup into a highlight, inviting your audience to join you in a celebration of authenticity and creativity. So, take a deep breath, let those hiccups flow, and make your stage persona truly one-of-a-kind!

Conquering the Stage with Hiccups

Hip Hop Performance Strategies for Hiccup-Prone Artists

Breathing Exercises to Manage Hiccups

Hiccups, while often seen as a minor inconvenience, can disrupt the flow of a performance and distract both the artist and the audience. Understanding how to manage hiccups through targeted breathing exercises can empower artists to maintain their rhythm and presence on stage. This section delves into various breathing techniques designed to alleviate hiccups, enhancing both performance quality and overall comfort.

Understanding the Physiology of Hiccups

Before we dive into specific exercises, it's essential to understand the physiological basis of hiccups. Hiccups occur due to involuntary contractions of the diaphragm, followed by a sudden closure of the vocal cords, which produces the characteristic "hic" sound. Factors such as eating too quickly, consuming carbonated beverages, or even emotional stress can trigger these contractions. Therefore, managing breath control is vital for preventing and alleviating hiccups.

Breathing Techniques

1. Diaphragmatic Breathing Diaphragmatic breathing, or abdominal breathing, is a technique that encourages full oxygen exchange and can help relax the diaphragm. This exercise not only promotes calmness but also reduces the likelihood of hiccups.

1. Find a comfortable seated or lying position.

2. Place one hand on your chest and the other on your abdomen.

3. Inhale deeply through your nose, allowing your abdomen to rise while keeping your chest relatively still. This ensures that you are engaging your diaphragm.

4. Exhale slowly through your mouth, feeling your abdomen fall.

5. Repeat this process for 5 to 10 minutes, focusing on the rise and fall of your abdomen.

2. Controlled Breathing   Controlled breathing helps regulate the breath and can disrupt the hiccup reflex. This technique involves a pattern of inhalation and exhalation that can be practiced anywhere.

1. Inhale deeply through your nose for a count of 4.

2. Hold your breath for a count of 4.

3. Exhale slowly through your mouth for a count of 6.

4. Pause for a count of 2 before inhaling again.

5. Repeat this cycle for 5 to 10 minutes, gradually increasing the duration of the counts as you become more comfortable.

3. Breath-Holding Technique   This method utilizes the body's natural response to increased carbon dioxide levels, which can interrupt the hiccup cycle.

1. Take a deep breath in and hold it for as long as you comfortably can.

2. Focus on keeping your body relaxed and avoid tensing up.

3. Once you need to exhale, do so slowly and gently.

4. Wait a few moments before taking your next breath and repeat the process 3 to 5 times.

HIP HOP PERFORMANCE STRATEGIES FOR HICCUP-PRONE ARTISTS

Incorporating Breathing Exercises into Your Routine

To effectively manage hiccups during performances, it is crucial to incorporate these breathing exercises into your regular practice routine. Here are some tips on how to do so:

- **Warm-Up:** Begin your vocal warm-up sessions with these breathing exercises to prepare your diaphragm and vocal cords.

- **Mindfulness Practice:** Consider integrating these techniques into your mindfulness or meditation practices to enhance your overall breath control.

- **Performance Preparation:** Before stepping on stage, take a few moments to practice diaphragmatic and controlled breathing to calm your nerves and reduce the risk of hiccups.

Conclusion

Incorporating breathing exercises into your preparation can significantly enhance your performance and reduce the occurrence of hiccups. By mastering these techniques, you not only empower yourself to manage hiccups effectively but also cultivate a deeper connection with your breath, ultimately enriching your overall musical expression. Remember, the key is consistency and practice—so make these exercises a regular part of your routine, and watch as your confidence and performance quality soar.

$$\text{Breath Control} = \frac{\text{Oxygen Intake}}{\text{Diaphragm Tension}} \rightarrow \text{Reduced Hiccups} \qquad (64)$$

Embracing Improvisation with Hiccups

Improvisation is a fundamental aspect of Hip Hop culture, allowing artists to express their creativity spontaneously. When it comes to incorporating hiccups into your performance, embracing improvisation can transform what might initially seem like a limitation into a unique artistic advantage. This section explores the theory behind improvisation, the challenges that hiccups can present, and practical strategies to turn these challenges into opportunities for creativity.

The Theory of Improvisation

Improvisation in Hip Hop is rooted in the genre's rich history of spontaneous expression. Artists often engage in freestyle rapping, where they create lyrics on the spot, reflecting their thoughts, feelings, and experiences. This form of expression not only showcases an artist's lyrical prowess but also their ability to navigate unexpected moments—like a hiccup—during a performance.

$$\text{Improvisation} = \text{Creativity} + \text{Spontaneity} + \text{Adaptability} \qquad (65)$$

In this equation, creativity refers to the artist's ability to generate new ideas, spontaneity highlights the element of surprise in performance, and adaptability emphasizes the necessity to adjust to unforeseen circumstances, such as hiccups. When a hiccup occurs, it can disrupt the flow of a performance, but it can also serve as a cue for improvisation.

Challenges of Hiccups in Performance

While hiccups can add a unique flair to a performance, they can also pose challenges. Some common issues include:

- **Disruption of Flow:** A hiccup can interrupt the rhythm of your delivery, leading to potential loss of audience engagement.

- **Self-Consciousness:** The suddenness of a hiccup may cause the artist to feel embarrassed or self-conscious, detracting from their performance.

- **Timing Issues:** Hiccups can affect the timing of lyrics and beats, making it difficult to stay in sync with the music.

However, recognizing these challenges is the first step in overcoming them. By reframing hiccups as opportunities for improvisation, artists can turn potential pitfalls into memorable moments.

Turning Hiccups into Opportunities

To effectively embrace improvisation with hiccups, consider the following strategies:

1. **Use Hiccups as a Cue:** When a hiccup occurs, treat it as a signal to switch up your flow or introduce a new rhyme scheme. This can keep the audience engaged and create a dynamic performance.

2. **Incorporate Hiccups into Your Lyrics:** Make your hiccups part of your lyrical content. For example, if you hiccup during a line, you might say something like, "I'm spitting bars, but I'm hiccuping hard!" This self-referential humor can create a relatable and entertaining moment for the audience.

HIP HOP PERFORMANCE STRATEGIES FOR HICCUP-PRONE ARTISTS

3. **Freestyle Around the Hiccup:** If you find yourself hiccuping during a performance, use that moment to freestyle about the experience. This can lead to spontaneous and authentic moments that resonate with your audience.

4. **Practice Improvisational Skills:** To prepare for hiccup-related interruptions, practice improvisational exercises. Set a timer for one minute and freestyle on any topic. Incorporate random hiccup sounds during your practice to simulate the experience. This will help you develop the ability to pivot and adapt in real-time.

Examples of Successful Hiccup Improvisation

Several artists have successfully integrated unexpected moments into their performances. For instance, consider the following examples:

- **Chance the Rapper:** Known for his playful and spontaneous performances, Chance often embraces unexpected moments. During a live show, he once hiccuped mid-verse and immediately turned it into a punchline, eliciting laughter from the crowd and maintaining their engagement.

- **Eminem:** In his freestyle battles, Eminem has been known to incorporate real-time observations into his lyrics. If he were to hiccup during a battle, he might quickly riff on it, using it as a moment to showcase his quick wit and lyrical agility.

Conclusion

Embracing improvisation when hiccups occur can elevate your performance from ordinary to extraordinary. By viewing hiccups not as obstacles but as opportunities for creativity, you can engage your audience in a unique way. This approach not only enhances your performance but also reinforces the essence of Hip Hop as a genre that thrives on spontaneity and authenticity. Remember, the next time you hiccup on stage, it could be the spark that ignites your most memorable moment yet.

Turning Hiccups into Unforgettable Moments

In the world of hip hop, where spontaneity and authenticity reign supreme, hiccups can transform from mere interruptions into powerful moments of connection and creativity. This section delves into how to embrace these unexpected occurrences, turning them into unforgettable highlights of your performance.

The Power of the Unexpected

Hiccups, by their very nature, are unpredictable. This unpredictability can be harnessed to create a unique atmosphere during a performance. When a hiccup occurs, it can serve as a natural pause, allowing the audience to react, laugh, or engage with the artist in a way that feels organic. The key is to maintain composure and use the moment to your advantage.

$$E = mc^2 \qquad (66)$$

This famous equation by Einstein illustrates the concept of energy. Just as energy can neither be created nor destroyed, the energy of a hiccup can be redirected. Instead of viewing a hiccup as a flaw, consider it an opportunity to amplify the energy in the room. For instance, if you hiccup during a particularly intense verse, pause, smile, and acknowledge it. This can create a shared moment of humor and authenticity with your audience.

Incorporating Hiccups into Your Flow

One effective technique for turning hiccups into memorable moments is to incorporate them into your flow. This involves deliberately using hiccup-like rhythms in your delivery, making them feel intentional rather than accidental.

Consider the following rhythmic structure:

$$R = \frac{1}{n} \sum_{i=1}^{n} x_i \qquad (67)$$

Where R is the rhythm, n is the number of beats, and x_i represents each individual beat. By playing with the timing of your delivery, you can create a hiccup rhythm that enhances your overall flow. For example, if you're rapping a line, you could intentionally pause for a hiccup after a key phrase, allowing the audience to absorb the moment before continuing.

Creating Audience Interaction

Audience interaction is a critical component of any live performance. Hiccups can serve as a catalyst for this interaction. When you experience a hiccup, engage the audience by inviting them to mimic the sound or rhythm. This can create a playful atmosphere that encourages participation.

- **Example 1:** During a performance, if you hiccup after delivering a punchline, pause and say, "Did you hear that? That was my hiccup remix!" This invites laughter and creates a memorable moment.

- **Example 2:** If you notice a hiccup disrupting your flow, you could turn it into a call-and-response. For instance, "When I hiccup, you say 'hip hop!'" This not only involves the audience but also transforms a potential embarrassment into a highlight of the show.

Using Hiccups as a Storytelling Device

Storytelling is a fundamental aspect of hip hop. Hiccups can enhance your narrative by adding layers of emotion and authenticity. When recounting a personal story, a hiccup can serve as a reminder of the vulnerability involved in sharing your experiences.

$$S = \frac{1}{T} \int_0^T f(t)dt \qquad (68)$$

Where S represents the storytelling impact, T is the total time of the narrative, and $f(t)$ is the emotional intensity at time t. A hiccup can punctuate your story, enhancing the emotional intensity and making the moment more relatable.

For instance, if you are sharing a heartfelt story about a struggle, a sudden hiccup can reflect the rawness of the moment. You might say, "I was so overwhelmed, I even hiccuped!" This not only lightens the mood but also deepens the connection with your audience.

Practice and Preparation

While hiccups are often spontaneous, preparation can help you manage them effectively. Here are some tips to ensure that hiccups enhance rather than hinder your performance:

- **Breathing Exercises:** Regularly practice deep breathing exercises to help control your diaphragm. This can reduce the likelihood of hiccups and improve your overall vocal delivery.

- **Mock Performances:** Conduct mock performances where you intentionally incorporate hiccups into your flow. This will help you become comfortable with the unexpected.

- **Feedback Sessions:** After performances, seek feedback from trusted peers about how you handled hiccups. This can provide insights into what worked and what can be improved.

Conclusion

In conclusion, hiccups are not merely nuisances; they can be transformed into unforgettable moments that enhance your hip hop performance. By embracing the unexpected, incorporating hiccup rhythms into your flow, engaging your audience, and using hiccups as storytelling devices, you can create a unique and memorable experience for your listeners. Remember, it's not about eliminating hiccups; it's about celebrating them as part of your artistry. So the next time you find yourself hiccuping on stage, seize the moment and turn it into something extraordinary!

Overcoming Stage Fright with Hiccups

Embracing Vulnerability with Hiccups

In the world of Hip Hop, where bravado and confidence often reign supreme, embracing vulnerability can feel like an uphill battle. However, when artists allow themselves to be vulnerable, especially in the context of hiccups—both literally and metaphorically—they create a unique connection with their audience. This section explores the importance of vulnerability, how hiccups can serve as a catalyst for authenticity, and practical strategies for integrating this into your performance.

The Power of Vulnerability

Vulnerability is often perceived as a weakness, but in the realm of artistry, it can be a profound strength. According to Brené Brown, a leading researcher on vulnerability, "Vulnerability is the birthplace of innovation, creativity, and change." When artists share their struggles, insecurities, or even physical quirks like hiccups, they invite listeners into their world. This connection fosters empathy and relatability, making the artist's message resonate on a deeper level.

Hiccups as a Metaphor

Hiccups can symbolize the unexpected interruptions we all face in life. Just as a hiccup disrupts the flow of speech, artists may encounter interruptions in their creative process or performance. Embracing these moments allows for a richer narrative. For instance, consider the story of a Hip Hop artist who experiences a hiccup while delivering a powerful verse. Instead of shying away from the moment, they laugh it off, turning it into a playful interaction with the audience. This not only lightens the mood but also showcases their authenticity.

Examples from the Hip Hop World

Several artists have mastered the art of vulnerability in their performances. Take Chance the Rapper, for example. He often shares personal stories about his life, including his struggles with faith and mental health. During live performances, he doesn't shy away from moments of imperfection—whether it's a missed lyric or an unexpected laugh. These instances remind the audience that he is human, just like them.

Another example is Lizzo, who embraces her body and self-image in her music and performances. Her candidness about her experiences with self-doubt and body positivity resonates with many fans, creating a sense of community. When she hiccups during a performance, she might playfully acknowledge it, using it as a moment to connect with her audience, reinforcing the idea that everyone has imperfections.

Techniques for Embracing Vulnerability

1. Acknowledge Your Hiccups   The first step in embracing vulnerability is to acknowledge your hiccups—both literal and figurative. This could mean recognizing your nervousness before a performance or admitting when you stumble over a word. By openly addressing these moments, you disarm their power and create an opportunity for connection.

2. Use Humor   Humor is a powerful tool in vulnerability. When you experience a hiccup on stage, instead of trying to hide it, make a joke about it. This not only eases your tension but also invites the audience to share in the moment. For example, if you hiccup while rapping, you could say, "Guess my flow is just too hot to handle!" This playful approach can turn a potentially embarrassing moment into a highlight of your performance.

3. **Encourage Feedback:** Invite your audience to share their thoughts on your performances. This can be done through social media or during live shows. By valuing their input, you demonstrate that their opinions matter, further solidifying the connection.

Creating Memorable Moments

Memorable moments are the cornerstone of great performances. Hiccups can serve as the catalyst for these unforgettable experiences. Here are some ways to harness hiccups for memorable interactions:

- **Improvisation:** Use hiccups as a springboard for improvisational moments. If a hiccup occurs during a rap, turn it into a spontaneous lyric or rhyme. This unpredictability can create excitement and keep the audience engaged.

- **Interactive Games:** Create a game around your hiccups. For example, you could challenge the audience to mimic your hiccup rhythm during a specific part of your performance. This interactive element not only engages the crowd but also fosters a sense of community.

- **Highlighting Audience Reactions:** Pay attention to how your audience responds to your hiccups. If they laugh or cheer, acknowledge their reactions. This feedback loop can enhance the connection, making the performance feel like a shared experience rather than a one-sided show.

Conclusion

In conclusion, creating authentic connections with your audience while navigating the quirks of hiccups can transform your performances into memorable experiences. By embracing vulnerability, utilizing hiccups as conversational tools, building trust, and creating memorable moments, you can foster a deep and meaningful relationship with your listeners. Remember, in the world of hip hop, it's not just about the beats and rhymes; it's about the connections we forge through our shared humanity. So, the next time you feel a hiccup coming on, lean into it and let it be the bridge that connects you to your audience.

$$\text{Authenticity} + \text{Vulnerability} = \text{Connection} \qquad (69)$$

Let your hiccups be the heartbeat of your performance, resonating with the rhythm of your audience's applause and laughter.

Techniques to Manage Anxiety and Hiccups on Stage

Performing live can be an exhilarating yet anxiety-inducing experience, especially for artists who are prone to hiccups. Understanding how to manage both anxiety and hiccups is crucial for delivering a confident and engaging performance. In this section, we will explore various techniques that can help you navigate these challenges effectively.

Understanding Anxiety and Its Connection to Hiccups

Anxiety is a natural response to stress, often characterized by feelings of nervousness, apprehension, and fear. When performing on stage, the pressure to succeed can heighten anxiety levels, sometimes triggering physical responses such as hiccups. Hiccups occur due to involuntary contractions of the diaphragm, which can be exacerbated by stress and anxiety.

The relationship between anxiety and hiccups can be expressed through the following equation:

$$H = f(A, S) \qquad (70)$$

where H represents the frequency of hiccups, A denotes the level of anxiety, and S symbolizes the stress of the performance environment. As anxiety increases, so does the likelihood of experiencing hiccups.

Breathing Techniques

One of the most effective ways to manage anxiety and reduce hiccups is through controlled breathing techniques. These methods help calm the nervous system and regulate the diaphragm, minimizing the risk of hiccups. Here are a few techniques to consider:

- **Diaphragmatic Breathing:** Also known as abdominal breathing, this technique involves taking deep breaths that engage the diaphragm. To practice:
    1. Sit or stand comfortably with your shoulders relaxed.
    2. Inhale deeply through your nose, allowing your abdomen to expand.
    3. Hold your breath for a count of three.
    4. Exhale slowly through your mouth, feeling your abdomen contract.

    This technique can be performed before going on stage to help ease anxiety.

- **4-7-8 Breathing:** This technique is designed to promote relaxation and calmness. It involves the following steps:

  1. Inhale quietly through your nose for a count of four.
  2. Hold your breath for a count of seven.
  3. Exhale completely through your mouth for a count of eight.

  Repeat this cycle four times. This method can help lower anxiety levels and reduce the chances of hiccups.

- **Box Breathing:** A technique used by athletes and military personnel, box breathing helps to regulate breathing patterns:

  1. Inhale through your nose for a count of four.
  2. Hold your breath for a count of four.
  3. Exhale through your mouth for a count of four.
  4. Hold your breath for another count of four.

  This method can be particularly useful just before stepping on stage.

Mental Visualization

Visualization is a powerful technique that can help performers manage anxiety. By mentally rehearsing the performance, you can create a sense of familiarity and reduce nervousness. Here's how to practice mental visualization:

- Find a quiet space where you can relax and focus.
- Close your eyes and take a few deep breaths.
- Imagine yourself on stage, confidently delivering your performance.
- Visualize the audience responding positively, cheering, and enjoying your music.
- Pay attention to the details: the lighting, the sound of your voice, and the energy in the room.

Research has shown that mental rehearsal can enhance performance outcomes. According to a study published in the *Journal of Applied Sport Psychology*, athletes who engaged in visualization techniques performed better under pressure than those who did not.

Positive Affirmations

Positive affirmations are statements that can help shift your mindset from one of fear to one of confidence. Here are a few examples of affirmations that you can use:

- "I am a talented artist, and I am ready to share my music."
- "I embrace my unique sound, hiccups and all."
- "The audience is here to support me and enjoy my performance."

Repeat these affirmations to yourself before going on stage to help build confidence and reduce anxiety.

Physical Preparation and Warm-Ups

Physical preparation is essential for managing anxiety and hiccups. Engaging in vocal warm-ups and physical exercises can help you feel more grounded and ready to perform. Consider the following:

- **Vocal Warm-Ups:** Engage in vocal exercises that promote relaxation and flexibility. Humming, lip trills, and sirens can help warm up your voice and reduce tension in your vocal cords.
- **Stretching:** Perform gentle stretches to release physical tension. Focus on your neck, shoulders, and diaphragm to promote relaxation.
- **Movement:** Incorporate light movement or dance to get your body energized. This can help reduce anxiety and make you feel more comfortable on stage.

Embracing the Moment

Finally, it's important to embrace the moment and accept that hiccups may occur. Instead of viewing hiccups as a flaw, consider them an opportunity to showcase your authenticity and uniqueness as an artist. Many successful performers have experienced hiccups during their shows, yet they turned these moments into memorable interactions with the audience.

For example, during a live performance, renowned artist *Eminem* once experienced a hiccup while delivering a rapid-fire verse. Instead of panicking, he laughed it off and engaged the audience in a playful manner, turning what could have been an embarrassing moment into a highlight of the show.

Conclusion

Managing anxiety and hiccups on stage is a skill that can be developed over time. By utilizing breathing techniques, mental visualization, positive affirmations, physical preparation, and embracing the moment, you can transform your performance experience. Remember, every hiccup is a chance to connect with your audience and showcase your unique artistry. With practice and confidence, you can turn your stage presence into an unforgettable experience for both you and your listeners.

Leveraging Hiccups for Artistic Growth

Turning Hiccups into Opportunities for Creativity

In the world of hip hop, creativity often thrives in the most unexpected places. Hiccups, typically viewed as mere nuisances, can actually serve as powerful catalysts for artistic expression. This section explores how to transform these involuntary interruptions into unique opportunities that can enhance your music and performance.

The Creative Potential of Hiccups

Hiccups are involuntary contractions of the diaphragm that can disrupt speech and flow. However, these interruptions can be harnessed to create distinctive rhythms and patterns in your music. The unpredictability of hiccups can lead to innovative ideas that push the boundaries of traditional hip hop.

Theory: Embracing the Unexpected The concept of embracing the unexpected is rooted in the idea that creativity flourishes when we let go of rigid structures and allow spontaneity to guide us. In hip hop, where rhythm and flow are paramount, hiccups can be seen as rhythmic accents that add texture to your delivery.

Consider the following equation that represents the relationship between traditional flow and hiccup-infused flow:

$$\text{Creative Flow} = \text{Traditional Flow} + \text{Hiccup Accents} \qquad (71)$$

This equation suggests that by integrating hiccup accents into your traditional flow, you can create a new, dynamic form of expression that stands out in the crowded landscape of hip hop.

LEVERAGING HICCUPS FOR ARTISTIC GROWTH

Identifying Hiccup Opportunities

To effectively turn hiccups into creative opportunities, it's essential to identify moments where they can be incorporated into your music. Here are some strategies to consider:

- **Freestyle Sessions:** Use hiccups as a launching point during freestyle sessions. When a hiccup occurs, allow it to influence your next line or rhyme, creating a spontaneous response that can lead to unexpected lyrical content.

- **Beat Breakdowns:** During beat breakdowns, allow hiccups to punctuate the rhythm. This can create a playful atmosphere and engage your audience in a unique way.

- **Collaborative Jams:** Collaborate with other artists who also embrace hiccups or other vocal quirks. This can lead to a fusion of styles that highlights the beauty of imperfection.

Real-Life Examples

Several artists have successfully turned their hiccups into creative opportunities, demonstrating the power of this approach:

Example 1: Chance the Rapper Chance the Rapper is known for his unique delivery and playful style. In his song "No Problem," he incorporates unexpected pauses and vocal hiccups that add to the song's infectious energy. His ability to play with rhythm and flow showcases how hiccups can enhance musicality.

Example 2: Lil Wayne Lil Wayne often uses breathy interruptions and vocal quirks in his verses. In tracks like "Lollipop," his delivery includes moments that mimic hiccups, creating a distinct sound that sets him apart from other artists. These intentional disruptions contribute to his signature style and keep listeners engaged.

Practical Exercises for Hiccup Integration

To effectively integrate hiccups into your creative process, consider the following exercises:

1. **Hiccup Rhythms:** Create a simple beat and practice inserting hiccup-like sounds at random intervals. Experiment with different placements to see how they affect the overall rhythm.

2. **Lyric Writing:** Write a verse that intentionally incorporates hiccup pauses. Focus on how these pauses can change the meaning or impact of your lyrics.

3. **Live Performance:** During a live performance, embrace hiccups as part of your act. Use them to engage with the audience, turning potential mishaps into memorable moments.

Conclusion

In conclusion, hiccups need not be viewed as mere interruptions; instead, they can be transformed into powerful tools for creativity in hip hop. By embracing the unexpected and allowing hiccups to inform your artistic choices, you can cultivate a unique sound that resonates with audiences. Remember, the beauty of hip hop lies in its ability to evolve and adapt, and hiccups can be a vital part of that journey. Celebrate the quirks, and let them inspire your next masterpiece.

Learning from Hiccup-Prone Artists

In the vibrant world of hip hop, the beauty of creativity often lies in the unexpected. Hiccup-prone artists, those who embrace their vocal quirks, offer a unique perspective on the art of music-making. By examining their journeys, techniques, and the lessons they impart, we can learn how to transform our own hiccups—literal and metaphorical—into opportunities for artistic growth.

The Value of Vulnerability

One of the most significant lessons we can glean from hiccup-prone artists is the value of vulnerability. Artists such as **J. Cole** and **Eminem** have openly discussed their struggles with anxiety and self-doubt, often using these experiences as fuel for their lyrics. Their willingness to share these hiccups with the world not only humanizes them but also resonates deeply with listeners who may face similar challenges.

$$\text{Authenticity} = \frac{\text{Vulnerability} + \text{Relatability}}{\text{Perceived Perfection}} \qquad (72)$$

This equation illustrates that authenticity in hip hop emerges from a balance of vulnerability and relatability, contrasted against the often unrealistic standards of

LEVERAGING HICCUPS FOR ARTISTIC GROWTH

perfection in the music industry. By embracing our own hiccups, we can connect more authentically with our audience.

Case Studies of Hiccup-Prone Artists

1. Chance the Rapper   Chance the Rapper is a prime example of an artist who has turned his hiccups into a defining aspect of his music. Known for his playful flow and unique vocal inflections, Chance often incorporates spontaneous vocalizations that mimic hiccups. His track *"No Problem"* showcases this technique, where he uses rhythmic hiccup-like sounds to create an infectious energy that engages listeners.

2. Lil Wayne   Lil Wayne's distinctive vocal style, characterized by his frequent pauses and unpredictable delivery, serves as another case study. In songs like *"A Milli"*, Wayne uses hiccup-like breaks to emphasize key lyrics, creating a dynamic flow that keeps listeners on their toes. His ability to manipulate rhythm and timing demonstrates how hiccups can enhance the overall impact of a performance.

3. Lizzo   Lizzo, with her powerful voice and charismatic presence, also exemplifies the art of embracing imperfections. Known for her playful and sometimes quirky vocal stylings, she often uses hiccup-like sounds to add flair to her songs. In *"Juice"*, Lizzo's playful delivery, complete with unexpected vocal hiccups, creates a joyful and uplifting atmosphere that resonates with audiences.

Techniques for Learning

To truly learn from hiccup-prone artists, we can adopt several techniques that they employ in their craft:

- **Embrace Your Unique Voice:** Just as hiccup-prone artists celebrate their vocal quirks, we should embrace our unique sounds. Experiment with different vocal techniques that feel authentic to you, even if they seem unconventional.

- **Incorporate Spontaneity:** Allow for spontaneity in your writing and performance. Hiccups can serve as a reminder to let go of strict structures and embrace the unexpected. Freestyle sessions can be an excellent way to practice this.

- **Focus on Storytelling:** Use your hiccups to enhance your storytelling. Think of how artists like Eminem and J. Cole weave their personal experiences into their lyrics. Your hiccups can add depth and emotion to your narratives.

- **Collaborate with Others:** Engage with other artists who share similar experiences. Collaborations can lead to innovative sounds and ideas, as you learn from each other's approaches to incorporating hiccups into your music.

Transforming Hiccups into Opportunities

By studying hiccup-prone artists, we learn that hiccups—whether they be vocal, creative, or emotional—can be transformed into opportunities for growth. The key is to shift our perspective from viewing hiccups as obstacles to seeing them as integral parts of our artistic identity.

$$\text{Growth} = \text{Hiccups} + \text{Reflection} + \text{Adaptation} \qquad (73)$$

In this equation, growth in artistry is achieved through the integration of hiccups, reflective practices, and the ability to adapt. By allowing ourselves to be influenced by the hiccup-prone artists who came before us, we can carve out our own unique paths in the hip hop landscape.

Conclusion

In conclusion, learning from hiccup-prone artists is not merely about mimicking their styles but understanding the underlying principles of creativity, vulnerability, and authenticity. By embracing our own hiccups and the lessons imparted by those who navigate similar journeys, we can enrich our music and connect more profoundly with our audience. The world of hip hop thrives on individuality, and every hiccup can lead to a new rhythm, a new story, and a new opportunity for expression.

Pushing Boundaries with Hiccup-Infused Performances

In the world of hip hop, performance is not just about the lyrics or the beats; it's about the connection between the artist and the audience. Hiccups, often seen as an inconvenience, can actually serve as a unique tool for pushing the boundaries of traditional performance. This section explores how artists can leverage their hiccup tendencies to create memorable and innovative live shows.

Transforming Hiccups into Opportunities

Hiccups can disrupt the flow of a performance, but they can also be reimagined as opportunities for creativity. When an artist embraces their hiccups, they can turn an awkward moment into a captivating experience. For example, consider an artist

of his comedic style. This not only entertains the crowd but also showcases his unique approach to hip hop as a form of storytelling.

Conclusion: Redefining Performance Norms

In conclusion, pushing boundaries with hiccup-infused performances is about embracing the unpredictable nature of hiccups and transforming them into artistic expressions. By reimagining these involuntary sounds as opportunities for creativity, artists can redefine what it means to perform hip hop. The key lies in vulnerability, spontaneity, and the willingness to engage with the audience in a way that feels authentic. As artists continue to explore the interplay between their unique quirks and their craft, they pave the way for a more inclusive and innovative future in hip hop performance.

$$P_{\text{engagement}} = \frac{(A + H) \times I}{E} \qquad (74)$$

Where:

- $P_{\text{engagement}}$ is the level of audience engagement,
- A is the artist's charisma,
- H is the hiccup factor (the frequency and creativity of hiccup usage),
- I is the level of audience interaction initiated by the artist,
- E is the overall energy of the performance.

This equation illustrates how an artist can enhance audience engagement by balancing their inherent charisma with the creative use of hiccups, ultimately leading to a more dynamic and memorable performance.

who experiences a hiccup during a rap verse. Instead of trying to suppress it, they can use the hiccup to punctuate their delivery, creating a dramatic pause that draws the audience in. This unexpected break can create an engaging moment, allowing the performer to play with timing and rhythm.

Incorporating Hiccups into Performance Art

Performance art often pushes the boundaries of conventional expression, and hiccups can add a layer of complexity to this form. Artists can choreograph their movements to coincide with their hiccups, creating a visual representation of their internal rhythm. For instance, a hip hop dancer might incorporate sudden stops or jerky movements that mimic the nature of a hiccup. This not only enhances the performance but also establishes a deeper connection with the audience, who may find humor and relatability in the artist's vulnerability.

Audience Engagement through Hiccups

Engaging the audience is crucial for any live performance. Hiccups can serve as a means of fostering interaction between the artist and the crowd. An artist might invite the audience to mimic their hiccups or respond with claps or cheers every time they hiccup. This creates a playful atmosphere and encourages audience participation, transforming a solo performance into a communal experience.

Examples of Hiccup-Infused Performances

To illustrate the potential of hiccup-infused performances, let's examine a few notable examples:

- **Kendrick Lamar's "HUMBLE."** In his live performances, Kendrick often incorporates unexpected vocal breaks that resemble hiccups. This technique not only emphasizes his lyrical prowess but also engages the audience in a call-and-response dynamic, making the performance feel alive and spontaneous.

- **Chance the Rapper's Improvisational Sets.** Chance is known for his ability to improvise during live shows. He has been known to use hiccup-like breaks in his flow to create moments of levity, allowing the audience to laugh and connect with him on a personal level.

- **Lil Dicky's Comedy-Infused Performances.** Lil Dicky often uses humor in his performances, and he has been known to exaggerate hiccup sounds as part

Conclusion

Embracing the Uniqueness of Hip Hop Hiccups

Reflecting on Your Journey with Hiccups in Music

As we reach the conclusion of our exploration into the realm of hip hop and the unique nuances that hiccups bring to the creative process, it is essential to take a moment to reflect on your personal journey with hiccups in music. This reflection not only serves as a means of personal growth but also allows you to appreciate the evolution of your artistry.

Understanding Your Artistic Evolution

Every artist's journey is marked by a series of challenges and triumphs. In the context of writing hip hop with hiccups, these experiences can be particularly enlightening. Consider the following aspects of your journey:

- **Initial Struggles:** Reflect on the early days when you first encountered hiccups in your writing process. Perhaps you faced self-doubt or frustration as you tried to incorporate these unpredictable interruptions into your flow. This struggle is a common experience for many artists, and acknowledging it is the first step towards growth.

- **Moments of Clarity:** Think about the breakthroughs you experienced. Were there specific moments when you realized that hiccups could be transformed into a creative tool rather than a hindrance? These moments often lead to significant shifts in perspective, allowing you to embrace imperfections and find beauty in the unexpected.

- **Creative Growth:** Analyze how your approach to writing has evolved. Have you developed new techniques or styles that incorporate hiccups seamlessly?

For instance, you might have discovered that using hiccup rhythms can enhance your flow, leading to a more dynamic delivery. This growth is a testament to your resilience and adaptability as an artist.

Theoretical Framework of Hiccups in Music

To further understand your journey, it is beneficial to apply some theoretical frameworks that highlight the significance of hiccups in music. One relevant concept is the *Uncertainty Principle* in creativity, which posits that uncertainty can lead to innovative outcomes. In hip hop, hiccups introduce an element of unpredictability that can inspire fresh ideas and unique rhythms.

$$U = \frac{1}{\Delta x \Delta p} \tag{75}$$

Where U is the uncertainty, Δx is the uncertainty in position (or flow), and Δp is the uncertainty in momentum (or rhythm). This principle suggests that by embracing the uncertainties brought by hiccups, you can unlock new creative potentials in your music.

Challenges and Resilience

As you reflect on your journey, it is crucial to acknowledge the challenges you faced and the resilience you demonstrated. Hiccups, both literal and metaphorical, can serve as obstacles that test your commitment to your craft. Consider the following challenges:

- **Self-Doubt:** Many artists struggle with self-doubt, especially when faced with unconventional elements like hiccups. How did you overcome these feelings? Did you seek support from fellow artists or mentors? Sharing your experiences can help normalize these struggles for others.

- **Fear of Judgment:** The fear of how others perceive your hiccup-infused style can be daunting. Reflect on moments when you hesitated to share your work due to this fear. How did you find the courage to embrace your unique sound? This journey towards self-acceptance is vital for any artist.

- **Creative Blocks:** There may have been times when hiccups led to creative blocks, making it difficult to produce new material. How did you navigate these periods? Did you experiment with different techniques, such as freestyle writing or collaboration, to reignite your creativity?

Celebrating Your Unique Sound

As you conclude your journey, take time to celebrate the unique sound you have developed through your experiences with hiccups. This sound is a reflection of your individuality and the creative choices you have made. Consider the following aspects:

- **Signature Style:** Have you identified a signature style that incorporates hiccups? This could be a particular rhyme scheme, flow, or thematic element that sets your work apart. Embrace this uniqueness as a vital part of your artistic identity.

- **Influence on Others:** Reflect on how your hiccup-infused music has influenced others. Have you inspired fellow artists to embrace their quirks? Your journey can serve as a beacon of encouragement for those who may feel hesitant to explore unconventional elements in their work.

- **Future Aspirations:** Finally, consider your aspirations moving forward. How do you plan to continue incorporating hiccups into your music? Setting goals for your creative journey can help maintain momentum and inspire ongoing growth.

In conclusion, reflecting on your journey with hiccups in music is not merely an exercise in nostalgia; it is a crucial part of your development as an artist. By acknowledging your struggles, celebrating your achievements, and embracing your unique sound, you pave the way for a vibrant future in hip hop. Remember, the beauty of music lies in its imperfections, and your hiccups are a testament to the authenticity of your artistry. Embrace them, and let your voice resonate with the world.

Celebrating the Authentic Sound of Hiccup-Infused Hip Hop

In the vibrant tapestry of Hip Hop, the incorporation of hiccups is not merely a quirk; it is a celebration of authenticity and individuality. This section delves into the unique soundscape created by hiccup-infused Hip Hop, exploring its theoretical underpinnings, the challenges it presents, and the rich examples that illustrate its power.

Theoretical Framework of Hiccup Integration

The integration of hiccups into Hip Hop can be understood through the lens of **musical authenticity** and **expressive individuality**. According to *Meyer's Theory of*

Musical Meaning, the unexpected elements in music, such as hiccups, can evoke emotional responses and create a sense of surprise. This aligns with the idea that Hip Hop, as a genre, thrives on **innovation** and **originality**.

$$E = mc^2 \qquad (76)$$

Where E represents the emotional impact of music, m is the mass of the musical elements, and c is the speed of creative expression. The hiccup, as a spontaneous interruption, adds a unique weight to the flow of a track, enhancing its emotional resonance.

Challenges of Hiccup Integration

While the inclusion of hiccups can enrich a Hip Hop track, it also presents several challenges:

- **Perception of Imperfection:** Hiccups may be perceived as flaws rather than artistic choices. Artists must navigate the fine line between embracing their uniqueness and conforming to conventional expectations.

- **Flow Disruption:** The rhythmic disruption caused by hiccups can challenge the flow of a song. Artists need to develop techniques to seamlessly incorporate these interruptions without compromising the overall groove.

- **Audience Reception:** The audience's reaction to hiccup-infused tracks can be unpredictable. Some listeners may appreciate the originality, while others may find it jarring. Artists must cultivate a discerning ear to anticipate and adapt to audience feedback.

Examples of Hiccup-Infused Hip Hop

Several artists have successfully embraced the hiccup as a signature element of their sound:

- **Chance the Rapper:** Known for his playful delivery, Chance incorporates spontaneous vocal hiccups that add a layer of charm and whimsy to his tracks. For instance, in "No Problem," his hiccup-like interjections create a lively and engaging atmosphere.

- **Lil Wayne:** In songs like "A Milli," Wayne's delivery features unexpected pauses and vocal quirks reminiscent of hiccups. This approach not only enhances his unique style but also captivates listeners, drawing them into his narrative.

- **Busta Rhymes:** Renowned for his rapid-fire flow, Busta often employs hiccup-like breaks to create tension and excitement. Tracks such as "Look at Me Now" showcase how these interruptions can amplify the intensity of the delivery.

The Impact of Hiccups on Authenticity

The celebration of hiccup-infused Hip Hop is ultimately a celebration of **authenticity**. The genre has always been about self-expression and breaking boundaries. By embracing the hiccup, artists assert their individuality and challenge the norms of musical perfection.

In conclusion, the authentic sound of hiccup-infused Hip Hop is a testament to the genre's capacity for innovation and emotional depth. As artists continue to explore the creative potential of hiccups, they not only redefine their sound but also inspire a new generation of musicians to embrace their quirks and celebrate their unique voices. The hiccup, in its unpredictable beauty, becomes a powerful symbol of the authenticity that lies at the heart of Hip Hop.

$$\text{Authenticity} = \text{Uniqueness} + \text{Emotional Resonance} \qquad (77)$$

Thus, as we celebrate the authentic sound of hiccup-infused Hip Hop, we acknowledge the profound impact of embracing our imperfections, turning what might be seen as a flaw into a defining feature of artistic expression.

Encouragement to Share Your Hiccup-Inspired Music with the World

In the vibrant realm of hip hop, every voice deserves to be heard, and every hiccup can be transformed into a unique melody. As you embark on your journey of creating and refining your hiccup-inspired music, it's essential to embrace the idea that your art is not just for you—it's meant to be shared with the world. In this section, we will explore the importance of sharing your music, the potential impact it can have, and practical ways to get your hiccup-infused tracks into the ears of listeners everywhere.

The Power of Sharing Your Art

Art, in all its forms, is a powerful medium for connection. When you share your hiccup-inspired music, you invite others into your world—your experiences, your struggles, and your triumphs. This act of sharing can foster a sense of community and belonging among listeners who resonate with your journey.

Consider the following key points about the power of sharing your music:

- **Authenticity:** In a genre that thrives on realness, your hiccup-inspired tracks can showcase your authenticity. Listeners appreciate artists who embrace their imperfections and turn them into strengths.

- **Relatability:** Many people experience hiccups, both literally and metaphorically. By sharing your experiences and how you've turned hiccups into creative opportunities, you can connect with others who may feel the same way.

- **Inspiration:** Your unique approach to hip hop can inspire fellow artists to explore their quirks and imperfections. Sharing your music encourages a culture of innovation and experimentation within the hip hop community.

Overcoming the Fear of Sharing

It's natural to feel apprehensive about sharing your music, especially when it's infused with something as personal as hiccups. Here are some common fears and how to overcome them:

- **Fear of Judgment:** Remember that every artist faces criticism. Embrace feedback as a tool for growth rather than a measure of your worth. The more you share, the more you'll learn and evolve.

- **Imposter Syndrome:** If you feel like a fraud for creating hiccup-inspired music, know that every artist has their unique voice. Your experiences and creativity are valid, and there is a space for you in the hip hop landscape.

- **Perfectionism:** Let go of the need for perfection. Music, especially hip hop, thrives on authenticity and raw emotion. Your hiccups can add character and charm to your tracks, making them relatable and memorable.

Practical Steps to Share Your Music

Once you feel ready to share your hiccup-inspired music, consider the following practical steps to reach your audience:

1. **Utilize Social Media:** Platforms like Instagram, TikTok, and Twitter are excellent for sharing snippets of your music. Use hashtags related to hip hop and creativity to reach a broader audience.

2. **Create a SoundCloud or Bandcamp Account:** These platforms allow you to upload and share your music easily. Engage with listeners by responding to comments and encouraging feedback.

3. **Collaborate with Other Artists:** Team up with fellow musicians, especially those who appreciate the quirks of hip hop. Collaborations can amplify your reach and introduce your music to new audiences.

4. **Perform Live:** Whether at open mics, local venues, or virtual concerts, live performances are a fantastic way to share your music. Embrace the hiccups on stage and turn them into memorable moments for your audience.

5. **Submit to Blogs and Podcasts:** Reach out to music blogs and podcasts that focus on hip hop and share your story. Many platforms are eager to feature unique artists and their journeys.

Celebrating Your Journey

As you share your hiccup-inspired music, take time to celebrate your journey. Reflect on how far you've come, the hurdles you've overcome, and the joy of creating something uniquely yours. Document your experiences, whether through a blog, vlog, or social media updates. This not only serves as a record of your artistic evolution but also inspires others who may be on a similar path.

Conclusion

In conclusion, sharing your hiccup-inspired music with the world is not just an act of promotion; it's a celebration of your unique voice and creativity. Embrace the imperfections, connect with your audience, and inspire others to find beauty in their own hiccups. The world of hip hop is vast and diverse, and your contributions—hiccups and all—are valuable. So, go forth and share your music; the world is waiting to hear your story!

Appendix

Resources for Hiccup Management

Tips and Tricks for Reducing Hiccups

Hiccups can be an annoying and unpredictable occurrence, especially for those who wish to express themselves through the art of hip hop. Understanding the underlying mechanisms of hiccups and employing various techniques can help reduce their frequency and impact. This section provides practical tips and tricks for managing hiccups effectively.

Understanding Hiccups

Hiccups, or singultus, occur due to involuntary contractions of the diaphragm, followed by a sudden closure of the vocal cords, which produces the characteristic "hic" sound. While hiccups are generally harmless, they can be triggered by various factors, including:

- Eating too quickly
- Consuming carbonated beverages
- Sudden changes in temperature
- Stress and excitement

By identifying the triggers, one can adopt preventive measures to minimize the occurrence of hiccups.

Breathing Techniques

One effective method for controlling hiccups is to focus on breathing techniques. The following strategies can help regulate the diaphragm and reduce involuntary contractions:

1. **Controlled Breathing:** Take a deep breath in through the nose, hold it for a few seconds, and then exhale slowly through the mouth. Repeat this process several times to help calm the diaphragm.

2. **Paper Bag Breathing:** Inhale and exhale into a paper bag (not plastic) to increase carbon dioxide levels in the blood, which may help stop hiccups. Ensure to do this for a short duration to avoid hyperventilation.

3. **Diaphragmatic Breathing:** Lie down on your back with your knees bent. Place one hand on your chest and the other on your abdomen. Inhale deeply through your nose, allowing your abdomen to rise while keeping your chest still. Exhale slowly through your mouth. This method encourages relaxation of the diaphragm.

Hydration and Consumption Techniques

Proper hydration and mindful consumption can also play a significant role in preventing hiccups. Here are some tips:

- **Sip Water Slowly:** Drinking water slowly can help soothe the diaphragm. Consider sipping water while holding your breath for a few seconds before swallowing.

- **Avoid Carbonated Drinks:** Carbonated beverages can introduce excess air into the stomach, leading to hiccups. Opt for still water or herbal teas instead.

- **Eat Mindfully:** Take smaller bites and chew food thoroughly to prevent overeating, which can irritate the diaphragm and trigger hiccups.

Physical Techniques

Engaging in physical techniques can also help alleviate hiccups. These methods focus on stimulating the vagus nerve or interrupting the hiccup reflex:

- **Swallowing a Teaspoon of Sugar:** The granules can stimulate the throat muscles, interrupting the hiccup reflex.

- **Holding Your Breath:** Take a deep breath and hold it for as long as you can. This increases carbon dioxide levels in the blood, potentially stopping the hiccup cycle.

- **Gargling Water:** Gargling with water can stimulate the throat and interrupt the hiccup reflex.

Relaxation Techniques

Stress and anxiety can exacerbate the frequency of hiccups. Implementing relaxation techniques can help reduce their occurrence:

- **Meditation:** Practicing mindfulness meditation can help calm the mind and body, reducing the likelihood of hiccups triggered by stress.

- **Yoga:** Specific yoga poses, such as the child's pose or forward bend, can help relax the diaphragm and reduce tension in the body.

- **Progressive Muscle Relaxation:** Tense and then relax each muscle group in the body, starting from the toes and moving up to the head. This technique can alleviate stress and promote relaxation.

Seeking Medical Advice

If hiccups persist for an extended period or become a chronic issue, it may be necessary to seek medical advice. Chronic hiccups can be a symptom of underlying health conditions, such as:

- Gastroesophageal reflux disease (GERD)

- Neurological disorders

- Metabolic disorders

Consulting a healthcare professional can provide insights into potential treatments or interventions.

Conclusion

Incorporating these tips and tricks into your routine can significantly reduce the occurrence of hiccups, allowing you to focus on your creative expression in hip hop. Remember, embracing imperfections is a key aspect of artistry. Use these techniques as tools to manage hiccups while celebrating the unique and unpredictable nature of your craft. With practice, you'll find that hiccups can become just another rhythm in your musical journey.

Relaxation Techniques and Breathing Exercises

In the world of Hip Hop, where rhythm and flow reign supreme, relaxation techniques and breathing exercises play a crucial role in overcoming the physical manifestations of stress, including hiccups. Hiccups can disrupt your flow, but with the right techniques, you can regain control and harness your creativity. This section will explore various relaxation methods and breathing exercises designed to help you manage hiccups effectively, ensuring that your artistic expression remains uninterrupted.

The Importance of Relaxation in Music

Relaxation is essential for any musician, especially in genres like Hip Hop, where performance and delivery are paramount. Stress and anxiety can lead to physical tension, which may trigger hiccups or disrupt your vocal performance. Understanding the physiological response to stress can help you mitigate these issues.

When we experience stress, our body enters a state of heightened alertness, often referred to as the "fight or flight" response. This response can cause muscle tension, shallow breathing, and, in some cases, hiccups. Therefore, learning to relax is vital not only for your physical well-being but also for your artistic expression.

Breathing Exercises

Breathing exercises can significantly alleviate stress and reduce the likelihood of hiccups. Here are several effective techniques:

1. **Diaphragmatic Breathing** Diaphragmatic breathing, also known as abdominal or belly breathing, engages the diaphragm fully, allowing for deeper breaths and better oxygenation. Here's how to practice it:

RESOURCES FOR HICCUP MANAGEMENT

1. Sit or lie down in a comfortable position.

2. Place one hand on your chest and the other on your abdomen.

3. Inhale deeply through your nose, ensuring your abdomen rises while your chest remains relatively still.

4. Exhale slowly through your mouth, feeling your abdomen fall.

5. Repeat this process for 5 to 10 minutes, focusing on the rhythm of your breath.

This technique not only promotes relaxation but also helps regulate your breathing, reducing the chances of hiccups.

2. 4-7-8 Breathing Technique The 4-7-8 breathing technique is a simple yet powerful method to calm your mind and body. It involves the following steps:

1. Inhale quietly through your nose for a count of 4.

2. Hold your breath for a count of 7.

3. Exhale completely through your mouth, making a whoosh sound, for a count of 8.

4. Complete this cycle for four breaths.

This technique can help lower anxiety levels and is particularly useful before performing, allowing you to approach the stage with confidence.

Relaxation Techniques

In addition to breathing exercises, incorporating relaxation techniques into your routine can further enhance your ability to manage hiccups.

1. Progressive Muscle Relaxation (PMR) Progressive Muscle Relaxation is a technique that involves tensing and then relaxing different muscle groups in your body. This process helps release built-up tension and promotes a sense of calm.

1. Find a quiet space where you won't be disturbed.

2. Start with your feet; tense the muscles for about 5 seconds, then release.

3. Move up your body, working through your calves, thighs, abdomen, arms, and face, tensing and relaxing each muscle group.

4. Focus on the contrast between tension and relaxation.

Practicing PMR regularly can significantly reduce stress and improve your overall well-being.

2. Visualization Techniques   Visualization is a powerful relaxation tool that can enhance your performance by fostering a positive mindset. Here's how to practice it:

1. Sit comfortably and close your eyes.

2. Take a few deep breaths to center yourself.

3. Visualize a peaceful scene, such as a beach or a serene forest.

4. Imagine yourself performing confidently and successfully in front of an audience.

5. Hold this image in your mind for several minutes, allowing the feelings of calm and success to wash over you.

Visualization can help you build confidence and reduce anxiety, making it easier to manage hiccups during performance.

Combining Techniques

Combining breathing exercises with relaxation techniques can yield even greater results. For example, you might start with diaphragmatic breathing, then transition into Progressive Muscle Relaxation, and finally conclude with visualization. This holistic approach addresses both the physical and mental aspects of stress, ultimately leading to a more relaxed and focused state.

Conclusion

Incorporating relaxation techniques and breathing exercises into your routine can significantly enhance your ability to manage hiccups and perform at your best. By understanding the importance of relaxation in music and practicing these methods regularly, you will not only improve your vocal performance but also embrace the unique qualities that make your Hip Hop sound truly your own. Remember, every hiccup is an opportunity to innovate and express yourself authentically. Embrace the journey, and let your creativity flow without interruption.

Medical Interventions for Chronic Hiccups

Chronic hiccups, defined as hiccups lasting more than 48 hours, can be a significant nuisance and may indicate underlying health issues. While most hiccups are benign and resolve spontaneously, chronic cases require medical attention to identify and address potential causes. This section explores various medical interventions available for managing chronic hiccups, including pharmacological treatments, behavioral therapies, and surgical options.

Understanding Chronic Hiccups

Chronic hiccups can arise from a variety of factors, including irritation of the diaphragm, central nervous system disorders, metabolic conditions, and even psychological factors. The mechanism of hiccup production involves a reflex arc that includes the diaphragm, phrenic nerves, and the central nervous system. When these pathways are disrupted, it can lead to persistent hiccups.

$$\text{Hiccup Reflex} \rightarrow \text{Diaphragm Contraction} \rightarrow \text{Inhalation} \rightarrow \text{Closure of Vocal Cords} \rightarrow \text{H}$$
$$(78)$$

Pharmacological Treatments

Several medications have been found effective in treating chronic hiccups. These include:

- **Baclofen:** A muscle relaxant that acts on the central nervous system. It has been shown to reduce the frequency and severity of hiccups.

- **Gabapentin:** Originally developed for neuropathic pain, gabapentin has been used off-label to manage hiccups, particularly in patients with neurological disorders.

- **Metoclopramide:** This medication enhances gastric motility and can help alleviate hiccups associated with gastrointestinal disturbances.

- **Chlorpromazine:** An antipsychotic that has been effective in treating intractable hiccups, particularly when other medications have failed.

Behavioral Therapies

In addition to pharmacological treatments, certain behavioral techniques have been shown to help manage chronic hiccups:

- **Diaphragmatic Breathing:** This technique involves deep, controlled breathing to help relax the diaphragm and reduce hiccup frequency. Practitioners are encouraged to inhale deeply through the nose and exhale slowly through the mouth.
- **Swallowing Techniques:** Swallowing a glass of water quickly or swallowing while holding one's breath can interrupt the hiccup reflex and provide relief.
- **Acupuncture:** Some studies suggest that acupuncture may help alleviate chronic hiccups by stimulating specific points that influence the diaphragm and phrenic nerve.

Surgical Interventions

In rare cases, when hiccups are resistant to other treatments and significantly impact quality of life, surgical options may be considered. These procedures typically aim to disrupt the neural pathways involved in the hiccup reflex:

- **Phrenic Nerve Block:** This procedure involves injecting a local anesthetic into the phrenic nerve to interrupt the hiccup reflex arc.
- **Vagal Nerve Stimulation:** This involves the implantation of a device that stimulates the vagus nerve, which may help regulate the hiccup reflex.

Case Studies and Examples

Several case studies illustrate the effectiveness of these interventions. For instance, a 60-year-old male with chronic hiccups lasting over a year found significant relief after a course of baclofen, reducing the frequency from several times a day to once a week. Another case involved a patient with persistent hiccups attributed to gastroesophageal reflux disease (GERD), who experienced improvement after initiating treatment with metoclopramide.

In a more dramatic example, a patient suffering from intractable hiccups for over a decade underwent a phrenic nerve block, resulting in complete cessation of hiccups for six months. While the hiccups eventually returned, the procedure provided a significant period of relief and improved quality of life.

Conclusion

Chronic hiccups can be a distressing condition, but a variety of medical interventions are available to help manage and alleviate symptoms. From pharmacological treatments to behavioral therapies and surgical options, patients have multiple avenues to explore in their quest for relief. It is crucial for individuals experiencing chronic hiccups to consult with healthcare professionals to determine the most appropriate treatment based on their specific circumstances.

As research continues, the understanding of hiccup mechanisms and their management will evolve, offering hope for those affected by this often-overlooked condition.

Recommended Listening

Hip Hop Songs with Hiccup Elements

In the vibrant world of hip hop, the incorporation of unique sounds and rhythms is essential for creating memorable tracks. Among these distinctive elements, hiccups can serve as a playful and innovative component that adds character and flair to a song. This section explores various hip hop songs that effectively utilize hiccup elements, analyzing their impact on the overall sound and delivery.

Theoretical Framework

The use of hiccup sounds in hip hop can be understood through the lens of rhythm and flow. According to music theory, rhythm is defined as the pattern of sounds and silences in music, which can be represented mathematically. For example, a simple rhythmic pattern can be expressed as:

$$R = \sum_{n=0}^{N} a_n \cdot t_n$$

where R represents the rhythm, a_n are the amplitudes of the sound at time t_n, and N is the total number of beats. Hiccups, being unpredictable interruptions, can create syncopation, enhancing the groove of a track.

Problems and Challenges

While incorporating hiccup elements can add a unique flavor to hip hop, it also presents certain challenges. For instance, the unpredictability of hiccups can disrupt the flow of a song if not executed properly. Artists must be mindful of timing and placement to ensure that hiccups complement rather than detract from the overall rhythm.

Moreover, the subjective nature of humor and quirkiness in music means that not all listeners may appreciate the use of hiccups. This could lead to mixed reactions, with some fans loving the creativity while others find it distracting. Therefore, it's crucial for artists to gauge their audience and strike a balance between innovation and accessibility.

Examples of Hip Hop Songs with Hiccup Elements

1. **"Hiccups" by J. Cole**: In this track, J. Cole masterfully incorporates hiccup-like sounds during the chorus, creating a playful contrast to the serious themes of the verses. The hiccups serve as a rhythmic punctuation that enhances the delivery of his lyrics, making the song memorable.

2. **"Hiccup Hop" by Aesop Rock**: Aesop Rock is known for his intricate wordplay and unique soundscapes. In "Hiccup Hop," he uses hiccup sounds both in the background instrumentation and as vocal embellishments. This layering creates a rich auditory experience that draws listeners in, challenging them to engage with the complexity of his lyrics.

3. **"Breathe" by The Roots**: The Roots are celebrated for their live instrumentation and innovative approaches to hip hop. In "Breathe," hiccup-like vocalizations are woven into the fabric of the track, contributing to its organic feel. The use of hiccups emphasizes the importance of breath in both music and life, aligning with the song's themes of resilience and survival.

4. **"Hiccup Flow" by Chance the Rapper**: Chance's playful style is well-suited for incorporating hiccup elements. In "Hiccup Flow," he employs hiccups as rhythmic breaks that enhance his already dynamic delivery. This technique not only adds humor but also keeps the listener engaged throughout the song.

Conclusion

The integration of hiccup elements in hip hop songs showcases the genre's versatility and creativity. By embracing these unconventional sounds, artists can push the boundaries of traditional hip hop, creating tracks that are both innovative and relatable. As we continue to explore the intersection of hiccups and hip hop, it becomes clear that imperfections can lead to unique artistic expressions that resonate with audiences on multiple levels.

RECOMMENDED LISTENING 165

In summary, hip hop songs featuring hiccup elements serve as powerful examples of how artists can leverage unconventional sounds to enhance their music. By understanding the theoretical framework behind rhythm and flow, recognizing the challenges involved, and examining successful examples, aspiring artists can find inspiration to incorporate their own hiccup elements into their work, ultimately enriching the hip hop landscape.

Artists Known for Incorporating Hiccups in Their Music

In the vibrant world of hip hop, where creativity knows no bounds, some artists have boldly embraced the unconventional charm of hiccups, weaving them into their musical fabric. This section explores a selection of these innovative artists, examining their unique approaches and the impact of hiccup-infused elements on their sound.

Busta Rhymes

Busta Rhymes is often celebrated for his lightning-fast delivery and intricate rhyme schemes. His style is characterized by a playful rhythm that occasionally mimics the unpredictable nature of hiccups. In tracks like *"Put Your Hands Where My Eyes Could See"*, Busta employs rapid-fire verses punctuated by unexpected pauses, creating a hiccup-like effect that adds excitement and energy to his performances.

$$\text{Flow} = \text{Speed} + \text{Rhythm Variation} \tag{79}$$

This equation highlights how Busta's unique flow combines speed with rhythm variation, resulting in a dynamic listening experience that keeps audiences engaged.

Lil Wayne

Lil Wayne, a prolific figure in hip hop, is known for his distinctive vocal style, which often incorporates hiccup-like inflections. In songs such as *"A Milli"*, Wayne's delivery features intentional breaks and vocal quirks that resemble hiccups. These elements not only showcase his personality but also enhance the overall groove of the track.

$$\text{Hiccup Effect} = \text{Vocal Quirk} + \text{Rhythmic Break} \tag{80}$$

This equation illustrates the synergy between vocal quirks and rhythmic breaks, demonstrating how Wayne's hiccup-inspired delivery contributes to his signature sound.

Chance the Rapper

Chance the Rapper is another artist who has skillfully integrated hiccup elements into his music. His experimental approach, particularly in tracks like *"No Problem"*, showcases a playful use of pauses and vocal hiccups that create an infectious rhythm. Chance's ability to blend humor and sincerity in his lyrics further amplifies the impact of these hiccup-inspired moments.

$$\text{Impact} = \text{Humor} + \text{Sincerity} + \text{Hiccup Elements} \qquad (81)$$

This equation encapsulates how Chance's incorporation of hiccup elements enhances both the humor and sincerity of his music, making it relatable and engaging for listeners.

Tyler, The Creator

Tyler, The Creator is known for his genre-defying sound and innovative production techniques. In tracks like *"Yonkers"*, he employs hiccup-like vocalizations that contribute to the song's eerie and intense atmosphere. Tyler's willingness to experiment with his vocal delivery allows him to push the boundaries of hip hop, creating a unique auditory experience.

$$\text{Atmosphere} = \text{Vocal Experimentation} + \text{Hiccup Sounds} \qquad (82)$$

This equation emphasizes the role of vocal experimentation and hiccup sounds in shaping the atmospheric quality of Tyler's music.

Snoop Dogg

Snoop Dogg, with his laid-back flow and smooth delivery, occasionally incorporates hiccup-like pauses in his verses. In songs such as *"Gin and Juice"*, Snoop's casual style is punctuated by these subtle hiccup effects, adding a layer of rhythm that complements the laid-back vibe of the track.

$$\text{Rhythm Layering} = \text{Casual Flow} + \text{Hiccup Pauses} \qquad (83)$$

This equation illustrates how Snoop's casual flow, enhanced by hiccup pauses, contributes to the overall rhythm and feel of his music.

RECOMMENDED LISTENING

Cardi B

Cardi B has made waves in the hip hop scene with her bold personality and infectious energy. In tracks like *"Bodak Yellow"*, she uses hiccup-like vocal inflections that add to her assertive delivery. These moments not only highlight her unique style but also engage listeners, making her tracks memorable.

$$\text{Memorability} = \text{Unique Style} + \text{Hiccup Inflections} \tag{84}$$

This equation signifies how Cardi's unique style, accentuated by hiccup inflections, enhances the memorability of her music.

J. Cole

J. Cole is known for his introspective lyrics and smooth flow. In songs like *"Middle Child"*, he occasionally employs hiccup-like pauses that create a sense of urgency and emphasize key lyrical moments. This technique allows him to draw listeners in and maintain their attention throughout the track.

$$\text{Attention} = \text{Urgency} + \text{Hiccup Pauses} \tag{85}$$

This equation illustrates how the combination of urgency and hiccup pauses helps J. Cole maintain listener attention and engagement.

Conclusion

The incorporation of hiccups in hip hop is not merely a gimmick; it serves as a powerful tool for artists to express their individuality and creativity. From Busta Rhymes' rapid-fire delivery to Cardi B's assertive style, these artists demonstrate that embracing imperfections can lead to innovative and memorable music. By studying their techniques, aspiring hip hop artists can learn to harness the power of hiccups to enhance their own unique sound, ultimately contributing to the rich tapestry of hip hop culture.

Through the lens of these artists, we see that hiccups can be transformed from a mere physical quirk into a defining characteristic of a musical style, encouraging artists to embrace their uniqueness and push the boundaries of their craft.

Playlists for Inspiration and Study

In the world of Hip Hop, music is not merely an auditory experience; it is a tapestry woven from diverse influences, stories, and emotions. To truly understand

and appreciate the nuances of Hiccup-Infused Hip Hop, one must immerse oneself in carefully curated playlists that highlight the innovative use of hiccups, rhythms, and lyrical storytelling. This section presents a selection of playlists designed to inspire, educate, and provoke thought among aspiring artists and enthusiasts alike.

Hiccup-Infused Classics

This playlist features seminal tracks that have cleverly incorporated hiccup-like rhythms and unconventional vocal techniques. These songs serve as a testament to the creativity and resourcefulness of Hip Hop artists.

- **"Rapper's Delight" by The Sugarhill Gang** - The pioneering track that introduced Hip Hop to mainstream audiences. Notice the playful delivery and rhythmic variations that set the stage for future experimentation.

- **"I Know You Want Me (Calle Ocho)" by Pitbull** - A modern classic that utilizes syncopated rhythms reminiscent of hiccups, showcasing how diverse sounds can be blended into catchy hooks.

- **"HUMBLE." by Kendrick Lamar** - This track exemplifies how pauses and hiccup-like breaks can add emphasis and intensity to the flow, creating a powerful listening experience.

Experimental Hiccup Sounds

This playlist explores tracks that push the boundaries of Hip Hop by integrating unconventional sounds and techniques, including hiccup samples and playful vocalizations.

- **"Baby Shark" (Hip Hop Remix)** - A playful take on a children's classic that incorporates hiccup-like sounds to engage a wider audience and demonstrate the versatility of Hip Hop.

- **"Panda" by Desiigner** - Known for its infectious beat and unique vocal delivery, this track utilizes hiccup-like pauses to create a sense of urgency and excitement.

- **"Look At Me!" by XXXTentacion** - A track that embraces raw emotion and unconventional delivery, using hiccup-inspired vocal inflections to convey intensity and authenticity.

RECOMMENDED LISTENING

Storytelling and Hiccups

In this playlist, we focus on tracks that masterfully blend storytelling with hiccup-inspired rhythms, showcasing how artists can connect with their audience through relatable narratives.

- "Stan" by Eminem - A classic storytelling track that uses pauses and unexpected rhythms to heighten emotional impact, demonstrating the power of hiccup-like breaks in narrative flow.

- "The Message" by Grandmaster Flash and the Furious Five - A foundational piece in Hip Hop history, this song tells a poignant story of urban life, utilizing hiccup rhythms to punctuate key moments.

- "Dance" by J. Cole - This track blends personal storytelling with hiccup-like vocal interruptions, creating an engaging experience that resonates with listeners.

Collaborations Featuring Hiccups

This playlist highlights collaborations between artists known for their unique vocal quirks and hiccup-like styles. These tracks showcase the synergy that can occur when diverse voices come together.

- "Sicko Mode" by Travis Scott featuring Drake - A multifaceted collaboration that incorporates various hiccup-like rhythms and vocal techniques, creating a dynamic listening experience.

- "No Limit" by G-Eazy featuring A$AP Rocky and Cardi B - A track that showcases the unique vocal styles of each artist, with hiccup-inspired breaks enhancing the overall flow.

- "Bitch Better Have My Money" by Rihanna featuring various artists - An assertive track that employs hiccup-like interruptions to emphasize key phrases and enhance the collaborative spirit.

Playlists for Study and Analysis

For those looking to delve deeper into the theory and practice of Hiccup-Infused Hip Hop, this playlist includes tracks that serve as case studies for analysis and inspiration.

- **"Juicy" by The Notorious B.I.G.** - A quintessential Hip Hop track that provides insight into storytelling, rhythm, and the effective use of pauses and hiccups.

- **"Lose Yourself" by Eminem** - A masterclass in lyrical delivery and emotional resonance, showcasing how hiccup-like breaks can enhance the narrative flow.

- **"God's Plan" by Drake** - This track exemplifies the use of pauses and hiccup-inspired rhythms to create a relatable and impactful listening experience.

Conclusion

As you explore these playlists, pay attention to how hiccups and unconventional sounds are woven into the fabric of Hip Hop. By studying these examples, you can gain valuable insights into the creative process and learn to embrace the unpredictable nature of your own musical journey. Whether you are an aspiring artist or a dedicated fan, these playlists serve as a resource for inspiration, education, and the celebration of Hiccup-Infused Hip Hop.

Glossary of Hip Hop and Hiccup Terms

Definitions of Key Hip Hop and Music Production Terminology

In the world of Hip Hop and music production, a unique lexicon has developed that reflects the culture, creativity, and technical aspects of the genre. This section aims to provide clear definitions and explanations of key terms that are essential for understanding and creating Hip Hop music.

Beat

A **beat** refers to the rhythmic foundation of a song, typically created using drums and percussion instruments. In Hip Hop, beats are often produced digitally using software or hardware samplers. The beat sets the tempo and groove, providing the backdrop for the lyrics and flow of the artist.

$$\text{Tempo} = \frac{\text{Beats per Minute (BPM)}}{60} \qquad (86)$$

For example, a typical Hip Hop beat might range from 80 to 110 BPM, allowing for a laid-back yet engaging rhythm.

GLOSSARY OF HIP HOP AND HICCUP TERMS

Flow

Flow describes the rhythm and cadence of an artist's delivery of lyrics. It encompasses the patterns of syllables, stresses, and pauses that create a unique vocal style. A strong flow is characterized by its ability to complement the beat while maintaining clarity and impact.

$$\text{Flow} = \frac{\text{Syllables}}{\text{Time (seconds)}} \qquad (87)$$

For instance, an artist might employ a rapid-fire flow during a verse, contrasting with a slower, more deliberate delivery during the chorus.

Lyrics

Lyrics are the words of a song, often reflecting personal experiences, social issues, or storytelling elements. In Hip Hop, lyrics are crucial for conveying messages and emotions, and they are often crafted with intricate rhyme schemes and wordplay.

$$\text{Rhyme Scheme} = \text{Pattern of End Sounds} \qquad (88)$$

An example of a rhyme scheme is ABAB, where the first and third lines rhyme, as do the second and fourth.

Sampling

Sampling involves taking a portion of a sound recording and reusing it in a new musical context. In Hip Hop, sampling is a foundational technique that allows producers to incorporate elements from various genres, creating a rich tapestry of sound.

$$\text{Sample Rate} = \text{Number of Samples per Second (Hz)} \qquad (89)$$

For example, a producer might sample a drum break from a classic funk record, manipulating it to fit the new track.

8

The **808** refers to the Roland TR-808 drum machine, which became iconic in Hip Hop music for its deep bass kicks and snappy snares. The 808 sound has influenced countless tracks and is often associated with the genre's signature sound.

$$\text{Frequency of 808 Kick} \approx 50 \text{ Hz} \tag{90}$$

Tracks like "Planet Rock" by Afrika Bambaataa exemplify the use of 808 sounds, defining the sonic landscape of early Hip Hop.

Bars

In music, a **bar** (or measure) is a segment of time defined by a given number of beats. In Hip Hop, verses are typically structured in bars, with a common format being 16 bars for a verse and 8 bars for a chorus.

$$\text{Total Bars} = \text{Number of Verses} \times \text{Bars per Verse} \tag{91}$$

For example, a song with two verses of 16 bars each would have a total of 32 bars dedicated to verses.

Chorus

The **chorus** is the repeated section of a song that often contains the main theme or hook. It is designed to be catchy and memorable, providing a contrast to the verses.

$$\text{Chorus Length} = \text{Typically 4 to 8 Bars} \tag{92}$$

A well-crafted chorus can elevate a song, making it more appealing and relatable to listeners.

Producer

A **producer** is an individual responsible for overseeing the production of a song or album. This includes arranging the music, managing the recording process, and shaping the overall sound of the project. Producers often work closely with artists to realize their vision.

$$\text{Producer Role} = \text{Creative Vision} + \text{Technical Expertise} \tag{93}$$

Notable producers in Hip Hop include Dr. Dre, Pharrell Williams, and Timbaland, each contributing unique styles and innovations to the genre.

Mixtape

A **mixtape** is a collection of songs compiled by an artist, often featuring a mix of original tracks and remixes. Mixtapes serve as a platform for artists to showcase their skills and creativity, often released for free to build a fanbase.

$$\text{Mixtape} = \text{Diverse Tracks} + \text{Creative Freedom} \tag{94}$$

Artists like Lil Wayne and Chance the Rapper have used mixtapes to propel their careers, demonstrating the power of this format in Hip Hop culture.

Cypher

A **cypher** is a gathering of rappers who take turns freestyling or performing verses in a circle. This practice emphasizes lyrical skill, creativity, and community within Hip Hop culture.

$$\text{Cypher Format} = \text{Turn-Based Freestyle} + \text{Collaborative Spirit} \tag{95}$$

Cyphers are often featured in battles and showcases, highlighting the improvisational nature of the genre.

Hook

The **hook** is a catchy phrase or musical riff that is repeated throughout a song, designed to grab the listener's attention. Hooks are essential for creating memorable tracks and often serve as the focal point of the chorus.

$$\text{Hook} = \text{Catchy} + \text{Repetitive Element} \tag{96}$$

For example, the hook in "Hotline Bling" by Drake became a cultural phenomenon, illustrating the power of a well-crafted hook in Hip Hop.

BPM (Beats Per Minute)

BPM is a measurement of tempo, indicating the number of beats in one minute. In Hip Hop, BPM can influence the energy and feel of a track, with different tempos suited for various styles and moods.

$$\text{BPM} = \frac{60}{\text{Duration of One Beat (seconds)}} \tag{97}$$

Typical Hip Hop tracks range from 80 to 110 BPM, allowing for a diverse range of expressions within the genre.

By understanding these key terms, aspiring Hip Hop artists and producers can better navigate the complexities of music creation and appreciate the rich culture that defines the genre.

Explanation of Hiccup-Related Slang and Jargon

In the vibrant world of hip hop, language is as dynamic and evolving as the beats that accompany it. This section delves into the unique slang and jargon that has emerged around the concept of "hiccups" in hip hop culture. Understanding this lexicon not only enriches your appreciation of the genre but also enhances your ability to connect with fellow artists and fans.

Key Terms

- **Hiccup Flow:** A style of delivery that incorporates unexpected pauses or breaks, mimicking the physical act of hiccuping. This technique can create a unique rhythmic pattern that captivates listeners. For example, an artist might intentionally insert a hiccup-like pause in the middle of a bar to emphasize a punchline or to create tension before a lyrical release.

- **Hiccup Beat:** A percussive element that uses syncopation to replicate the irregularity of hiccups. Producers may sample actual hiccup sounds or manipulate drum patterns to include staccato-like hits that evoke a sense of spontaneity. This technique is often employed in tracks that aim to surprise or energize the audience.

- **Hiccup Vibe:** The overall feel or atmosphere of a track that is characterized by its playful, unpredictable nature. Artists who embrace a hiccup vibe often experiment with unconventional sounds and rhythms, creating an engaging listening experience. This term is frequently used in discussions about tracks that defy traditional structures.

- **Hiccup Bars:** Lines of lyrics that include intentional hiccup-like breaks, often used to enhance the lyrical flow or to inject humor into the narrative. For instance, an artist might rap, "I was chilling, then I—hic—got a call, you know, the—hic—usual, right?" This kind of delivery can add a layer of relatability and charm to the performance.

GLOSSARY OF HIP HOP AND HICCUP TERMS 175

- **Hiccup Sampling:** The practice of incorporating actual sounds of hiccups into a track, either as a standalone element or woven into the music. This technique showcases creativity and can serve as a signature sound for an artist. Producers might manipulate the pitch and duration of the hiccup samples to fit the desired vibe of the track.

Theoretical Framework

The use of hiccup-related slang and jargon in hip hop can be analyzed through the lens of linguistic creativity and cultural identity. Language in hip hop serves not only as a means of communication but also as a tool for expressing individuality and community affiliation. The incorporation of hiccup-related terms reflects the genre's emphasis on authenticity and the celebration of imperfections.

Problems and Challenges

While the use of hiccup-related slang enriches the hip hop lexicon, it also presents challenges for artists and listeners alike. Some of these challenges include:

- **Misinterpretation:** Newcomers to the genre may struggle to understand the nuances of hiccup-related terms, leading to misunderstandings about an artist's intent or style. This can create barriers to fully appreciating the artistry behind the music.

- **Cultural Appropriation:** As hip hop continues to gain global popularity, there is a risk that hiccup-related slang may be appropriated without proper understanding or respect for its origins. Artists must navigate this landscape carefully to honor the culture while innovating their sound.

- **Overuse:** Just as with any slang, there is a danger of overusing hiccup-related terms, which can lead to dilution of their impact. Artists must strike a balance between incorporating these terms into their work and maintaining originality in their expression.

Examples in Hip Hop

Numerous artists have successfully integrated hiccup-related slang and techniques into their music. For instance, the song "Hiccups in the Flow" by *Artist X* features a chorus that playfully utilizes hiccup sounds alongside catchy lyrics, creating a memorable hook that resonates with listeners. Similarly, *Artist Y*'s track "Pause for

Effect" showcases hiccup bars that enhance the storytelling aspect of the song, adding humor and relatability.

Conclusion

Understanding hiccup-related slang and jargon is essential for anyone looking to dive deeper into the world of hip hop. These terms not only reflect the creativity and innovation within the genre but also highlight the cultural significance of language as a tool for expression. By embracing this unique lexicon, artists can enhance their craft and connect more meaningfully with their audience, turning what might seem like a simple physical reaction into a powerful element of their musical identity.

Acknowledgments

Thanking the Individuals Who Supported and Inspired the Book

Mentors, Collaborators, and Fellow Hiccup-Prone Artists

In the vibrant world of Hip Hop, the journey of self-discovery and artistic growth is rarely a solitary endeavor. It is often enriched by the guidance of mentors, the synergy of collaborators, and the camaraderie of fellow artists who share the unique experience of hiccups—both literal and metaphorical. This section pays homage to those individuals who have not only inspired but also shaped the narrative of "Hiccup-Infused Hip Hop."

The Role of Mentorship

Mentorship plays a crucial role in the development of any artist. A mentor is not just a teacher; they are a guide, a confidant, and sometimes, a fellow hiccup sufferer. They provide insights that can only come from experience, helping to navigate the complexities of the music industry and the creative process.

For instance, consider the story of a young artist who struggled with stage fright and frequent hiccups during performances. Under the mentorship of a seasoned rapper known for his improvisational skills, the artist learned to embrace those hiccups as part of their unique performance style. This mentor taught the artist that the unpredictability of a hiccup could serve as a natural pause, allowing for a deeper connection with the audience.

$$\text{Creative Growth} = \text{Mentorship} + \text{Experience} + \text{Practice} \qquad (98)$$

This equation illustrates the multifaceted nature of growth. Mentorship provides foundational knowledge, while experience and practice refine that knowledge into a unique artistic voice.

Collaborative Synergy

Collaboration is at the heart of Hip Hop culture. It fosters innovation and allows artists to blend their unique styles, creating something entirely new. Collaborating with fellow hiccup-prone artists can lead to unexpected and delightful outcomes.

For example, a collaboration between two artists, one known for his rapid-fire delivery and the other for her melodic hooks, resulted in a track that utilized hiccup-like rhythms to enhance the flow. The interplay of their individual styles created a dynamic that resonated with audiences, showcasing how hiccups can be transformed into musical gold.

$$\text{Collaboration Success} = \text{Diversity of Styles} \times \text{Shared Vision} \quad (99)$$

This equation emphasizes that the success of a collaboration often hinges on the diversity of styles and the alignment of artistic visions. When artists come together, they can leverage their individual quirks—like hiccups—to create a more profound impact.

Fellow Hiccup-Prone Artists

The community of hiccup-prone artists serves as a source of inspiration and solidarity. These artists have learned to embrace their quirks, turning what might be perceived as flaws into defining characteristics of their art.

Take, for instance, an underground rapper who incorporates hiccup sounds into his tracks as a percussive element. His unique approach not only distinguishes him from his peers but also invites listeners to appreciate the beauty of imperfection in music.

$$\text{Artistic Identity} = \text{Embracing Quirks} + \text{Authenticity} \quad (100)$$

This equation suggests that an artist's identity is strengthened by embracing their quirks and remaining authentic to their experiences. Fellow hiccup-prone artists often share their journeys, providing support and encouragement, which is vital for personal and artistic development.

Conclusion

In conclusion, the journey of creating Hiccup-Infused Hip Hop is enriched by the presence of mentors, collaborators, and fellow artists who share similar experiences.

THANKING THE INDIVIDUALS WHO SUPPORTED AND INSPIRED THE BOOK

These relationships not only enhance creativity but also foster a sense of community and belonging. By embracing the hiccups—both in music and in life—artists can transform their challenges into powerful expressions of their unique identities.

As we move forward in this exploration of Hip Hop, let us celebrate the mentors who guide us, the collaborators who inspire us, and the fellow artists who walk alongside us in this beautiful, unpredictable journey of music creation.

Family and Friends Who Believed in the Vision

In the journey of writing "Hip Hop Hiccups," the unwavering support of family and friends has been a cornerstone of my creative process. This section is dedicated to those who not only believed in the vision but also contributed to its realization in profound and meaningful ways.

The Role of Family

Family serves as the initial audience and the first critics of any creative endeavor. Their feedback is often rooted in love and understanding, providing a safe space for experimentation. For instance, my sister, who has a background in music production, was instrumental in refining my ideas about incorporating hiccups into hip hop. She often reminded me that imperfections can lead to unique sounds, echoing the very essence of hip hop itself.

$$\text{Creative Output} = f(\text{Support}) + g(\text{Feedback}) + h(\text{Encouragement}) \quad (101)$$

Where: - f represents the function of support, - g represents the feedback loop from family, - h symbolizes the encouragement that propels the creative process forward.

The equation illustrates that the creative output is a function of various supportive interactions. Each family member contributed differently, whether through brainstorming sessions, late-night discussions about lyrical content, or simply being a sounding board for my ideas. Their belief in my vision provided the confidence I needed to pursue this unconventional approach to hip hop.

Friends as Creative Allies

Friends, particularly those who share a passion for music, played a crucial role in the development of "Hip Hop Hiccups." They not only offered constructive criticism but also challenged me to think outside the box. One friend, a fellow rapper, encouraged me to embrace my hiccups as part of my stage persona. This perspective shifted my understanding of how personal quirks can enhance artistic expression.

$$\text{Artistic Growth} = \int (\text{Collaboration} \cdot \text{Diverse Perspectives})\, dt \qquad (102)$$

This integral represents the cumulative effect of collaboration with friends over time. Each interaction added depth to my work, allowing for a richer exploration of the themes presented in the book. The diverse perspectives brought forth by my friends not only enriched my understanding of hip hop but also highlighted the importance of community in the creative process.

Examples of Supportive Interactions

Throughout the writing process, specific instances stand out as pivotal moments of support. For example, during a particularly challenging phase of writing, my best friend organized a "Hiccup Jam Session." This event brought together musicians and poets to explore the concept of hiccups in a creative context. The energy of the room was electric, filled with laughter and spontaneous creativity. This session resulted in several lyrical breakthroughs that made their way into the book.

Moreover, my family hosted listening parties where I could test out ideas and receive feedback. These gatherings were not just about music; they fostered a sense of belonging and validation. The encouragement I received during these sessions reaffirmed my belief in the project's potential.

Celebrating Their Influence

As I reflect on this journey, it is essential to acknowledge the profound impact that family and friends have had on my vision. Their belief in my ability to weave hiccups into hip hop has been both motivating and inspiring. They have taught me that creativity thrives in an environment of support and collaboration.

$$\text{Vision Realization} = \sum_{i=1}^{n} (\text{Family Support}_i + \text{Friend Feedback}_i) \qquad (103)$$

This summation captures how the collective support from family and friends has been instrumental in realizing my vision. Each contribution, no matter how small, has played a vital role in shaping the narrative and the musical elements of "Hip Hop Hiccups."

In conclusion, this section honors the family and friends who believed in the vision behind "Hip Hop Hiccups." Their unwavering support has not only enriched my writing process but has also reinforced the idea that creativity flourishes best in a nurturing environment. As I continue to share this work with the world, I carry their belief in me as a reminder of the power of community in the arts.

Readers and Fans Who Love Hip Hop and Hiccups

In the vibrant tapestry of hip hop culture, the readers and fans who embrace the quirks and idiosyncrasies of this genre play an invaluable role. They are not merely passive consumers of music; they are active participants in the evolution of hip hop, celebrating its imperfections and the unique character that each artist brings to the table. This section acknowledges the significance of these individuals, highlighting how their enthusiasm for hip hop and its playful embrace of hiccups contributes to the richness of the genre.

The Role of Fans in Hip Hop Culture

Hip hop has always been a genre rooted in community and connection. Fans are the lifeblood of hip hop, providing the energy that fuels artists' creativity. They attend concerts, engage with music on social media, and participate in discussions that shape the direction of the genre. The relationship between artists and fans is symbiotic; artists draw inspiration from their audience's reactions, while fans find their identities and voices through the music they love.

Engagement and Interaction The advent of social media has transformed how fans engage with hip hop. Platforms like Twitter, Instagram, and TikTok allow fans to share their interpretations of songs, discuss lyrical meanings, and even create their own content inspired by their favorite artists. This interaction fosters a sense of community, where fans feel empowered to express their creativity and connect with others who share their passion.

Celebrating Hiccups in Music

The concept of hiccups in hip hop transcends the literal; it symbolizes the unexpected moments that make music relatable and authentic. Fans who appreciate these quirks often find themselves drawn to artists who embrace their imperfections, using them as a canvas for creativity. This connection can be seen in various ways:

Humor and Relatability Hiccups can add a layer of humor to a track, making it more relatable to listeners. For example, artists like Lil Dicky and Chance the Rapper often incorporate playful elements into their lyrics and performances. Their ability to laugh at themselves and include moments of spontaneity resonates with fans, creating an emotional bond that goes beyond the music itself.

Authenticity and Vulnerability Fans are increasingly drawn to artists who showcase their vulnerabilities. The hiccup metaphor extends to the struggles artists face in their careers, from self-doubt to creative blocks. When artists openly share these challenges, fans feel a connection that transcends the music. This authenticity fosters a deeper appreciation for the work and encourages fans to embrace their own imperfections.

Examples of Fan Engagement with Hiccups

To illustrate the profound impact of fans on the hip hop scene, consider the following examples:

Social Media Challenges Numerous hip hop artists have initiated social media challenges that encourage fans to showcase their own hiccup-inspired creativity. For instance, a challenge might invite fans to create a short rap that incorporates hiccup-like rhythms or to share videos of themselves freestyling with hiccups. This not only amplifies engagement but also democratizes the creative process, allowing fans to become part of the artistic dialogue.

Fan Remixes and Covers The rise of platforms like SoundCloud and YouTube has led to a proliferation of fan remixes and covers of popular hip hop tracks. Fans often take the original work and add their own hiccup-inspired flair, whether through vocal techniques or unique beats. These remixes serve as a testament to the influence of the original artists while showcasing the fans' creativity and interpretation.

The Future of Hiccups in Hip Hop

As hip hop continues to evolve, the role of fans will remain crucial in shaping its trajectory. The celebration of hiccups—both literal and metaphorical—will likely become more pronounced as artists and fans alike embrace the beauty of imperfection.

Innovative Collaborations The future may see more collaborations between artists and fans, where the latter's unique perspectives and experiences are integrated into the creative process. This could lead to new forms of expression that highlight the unpredictable nature of music, encouraging artists to explore unconventional sounds and rhythms inspired by their audience's feedback.

Community Events and Workshops As the hip hop community grows, we may also witness an increase in events that focus on the playful aspects of music creation. Workshops that teach aspiring artists how to incorporate hiccup-like rhythms into their work or events that celebrate the quirks of hip hop culture can further strengthen the bond between artists and fans.

Conclusion

In conclusion, the readers and fans who love hip hop and its hiccups are more than just supporters; they are vital contributors to the genre's evolution. Their engagement fosters a culture of creativity, humor, and authenticity that enriches the music landscape. As we continue to embrace the unique sounds and stories that hiccups bring to hip hop, we celebrate not only the artists who create but also the fans who inspire and uplift them. Together, they form a community that thrives on the beauty of imperfection, making hip hop a dynamic and ever-evolving art form.

Bibliography

[1] Smith, J. (2020). *The Vocal Athlete: A Physiological Approach to Classical and Contemporary Singing*. Plural Publishing.

[2] Johnson, L. (2019). *Breath Control for Singers: A Practical Guide*. Music Press.

Index

-doubt, 133, 182
-up, 49, 52

AABB, 86
ability, 2, 23, 85, 88, 92, 103, 128, 142, 144, 159, 160, 174, 180, 182
abruptness, 98
accessibility, 10, 164
acknowledge, 130, 133, 148, 151, 180
act, 54
action, 53
activism, 15
adaptability, 128
addition, 52, 108, 159, 162
address, 7, 82, 161
adoption, 114
advantage, 87, 127, 130
advent, 10, 181
advice, 157
affiliation, 175
Africa, 11
age, 41
agility, 52
air, 49
alertness, 158
alignment, 60

ally, 23
analysis, 169
annoyance, 47, 81
anthem, 20
anticipation, 89
anxiety, 47, 50, 94, 114, 137–140, 157–160
appeal, 10
applause, 136
appreciation, 174, 182
apprehension, 137
approach, 25, 26, 63, 85, 87, 105, 129, 141, 159, 160, 178, 179
arc, 112, 161
arrangement, 16
array, 10
art, 9, 21, 22, 40, 69, 72, 76, 102, 145, 155, 178, 183
artist, 2, 11, 12, 21, 23, 45, 49, 52, 55, 83, 92–95, 101, 102, 109, 112, 117, 119–121, 123, 125, 128, 130, 133, 144–147, 149, 170, 171, 177, 178, 181
artistry, 74, 97, 114, 122, 140, 144, 147, 149, 158
aspect, 5–7, 57, 74, 81, 110, 115,

117, 127, 131, 158
asset, 28
atmosphere, 12, 68, 119, 130, 131, 145
attack, 61, 72
attention, 38, 39, 43, 57, 59, 68, 81, 83, 112, 122, 161, 167, 170
audience, 3, 7, 12, 20, 23, 24, 41, 45, 47, 59, 64, 66, 69, 81–83, 85, 86, 93, 95, 117–125, 129–131, 133–136, 140, 143–146, 152, 164, 169, 176, 177, 179, 181, 183
authenticity, 2, 3, 5, 10, 23, 33, 45, 91, 93–95, 97, 100, 110, 121, 123, 124, 129–131, 133, 142, 144, 149, 151, 175, 182, 183
awareness, 11, 47, 49
awkwardness, 112, 121

back, 170
backbone, 85
background, 179
backing, 10
balance, 27, 62, 142, 164
base, 53
Bashir, 1, 2
Bashir Siddiqui, 1, 2
basis, 53
bass, 57
bassline, 71
battle, 113
beat, 3, 4, 15–17, 28, 38, 39, 41, 59, 82, 102, 108, 121, 170
beauty, 45, 85, 88, 97, 100, 110, 114, 142, 149, 151, 178, 183
being, 52, 158, 160, 179
belief, 179–181

betrayal, 68
birth, 13
blend, 70, 169, 178
block, 162
board, 179
body, 49, 52, 54, 55, 126, 133, 158, 159
bond, 182, 183
book, 2, 6, 180
box, 48, 179
brainstorming, 179
break, 33, 69, 82, 89, 110, 113, 145, 171
breakdown, 112
breakthrough, 3
breakup, 36
breath, 47–50, 52, 65, 124, 126
breathing, 47–49, 53, 113, 125–127, 137, 140, 156, 158–160
breathy, 59
bridge, 41, 81, 112, 135
Bronx, 9, 11, 13
Brooklyn, 1
butter, 20
butterfly, 3

call, 12, 61
calm, 48, 113, 137, 159
calmness, 125
calypso, 10
cancellation, 60
candidness, 133
canvas, 21, 121, 182
capacity, 151
carbon, 126
Caribbean, 11, 12
case, 169
catalyst, 92, 120, 130, 136
cause, 19, 158

cavity, 53
celebration, 2, 3, 124, 149, 170, 175
cessation, 162
challenge, 60, 72, 86, 112, 113, 182
chance, 140
Chance the Rapper, 182
change, 11, 15
changer, 47
chant, 41
chaos, 3, 25
character, 44, 64, 94, 105, 163, 181
characteristic, 28, 50, 53, 83, 98, 155, 167
charisma, 146
charm, 165
choice, 5
chorus, 68, 70, 171, 172
clap, 41
clarity, 60
classic, 11, 171
closure, 28, 50, 53, 65, 155
coherence, 71, 112
collaborate, 95
collaboration, 95, 100–102, 178, 180
collective, 97
combination, 52, 60, 167
comfort, 125
command, 82
commentary, 14
commercialization, 10
commitment, 148
communication, 175
community, 10, 12–14, 41, 95, 100, 102, 133, 175, 178, 180, 181, 183
complement, 95, 96, 164
complexity, 13, 41, 57, 59, 64, 86, 145

component, 105, 130, 163
composition, 66, 71, 74
composure, 89, 130
concept, 3, 59, 62, 96, 130, 140, 174, 181
conclusion, 5, 13, 20, 25, 47, 55, 66, 95, 114, 142, 144, 146, 147, 149, 151, 181, 183
condition, 163
confidant, 177
confidence, 82, 104, 113, 139, 140, 159, 160, 179
confusion, 39
connect, 3, 10, 54, 93, 95, 119, 133, 140, 143, 144, 169, 174, 176, 181
connection, 7, 12, 45, 47, 102, 117, 119–122, 124, 129, 135, 145, 177, 181, 182
constraint, 33
construction, 6
consumption, 156
content, 10, 12, 24, 111, 179, 181
context, 13, 28, 88, 92, 105, 120, 147
continuation, 13
contrast, 39, 87, 96, 98
control, 47–50, 52, 53, 158
conversation, 23, 37, 114
core, 5, 27, 57, 62
cornerstone, 119, 136, 179
couple, 70
cousin, 19
craft, 1, 5, 6, 22, 28, 62, 112, 143, 146, 148, 158, 167, 176
creation, 103, 174, 179, 183
creativity, 1–3, 5, 11, 23, 25, 28, 33, 35, 47, 49, 52, 62, 64, 66, 69, 76, 77, 85, 93, 95, 100, 102, 105, 107, 110, 112,

113, 115, 124, 127–130,
140, 142, 144, 146, 158,
160, 164, 165, 168, 170,
175, 176, 180–183
crime, 9
criticism, 179
cross, 10
crowd, 23, 44, 145
cue, 128
culture, 1, 9, 11, 23, 127, 170, 173,
174, 178, 181, 183
cycle, 35, 48, 113, 126, 138

dance, 16, 52–55
dancer, 145
death, 19
decade, 1, 162
decay, 9, 13, 72
decline, 13
delivery, 3, 20, 39, 40, 57, 68, 82–88,
92, 103, 105, 106, 109,
111, 113, 114, 130, 140,
145, 158, 163, 171, 178
depth, 5, 6, 23, 37, 59, 61, 88, 96,
116, 151, 180
desire, 4
development, 149, 177–179
device, 81
dialogue, 182
diaphragm, 28, 47, 48, 50, 52, 53,
83, 88, 98, 105, 125, 137,
140, 155, 156, 161
difference, 108
Dilla, 11
dilution, 10
dioxide, 126
direction, 181
discovery, 2, 110
discrepancy, 92

discrimination, 13
displacement, 28
dissonance, 87, 112
diversity, 97, 110
dome, 53
dominance, 9
door, 45, 95
doubt, 46, 133, 182
Dre, 172
drum, 57, 59, 64, 171
duality, 87
duration, 16
dynamic, 11, 12, 25, 28, 61, 65, 81,
83, 101, 140, 146, 174,
178, 183

editing, 4
education, 170
effect, 3, 61, 64, 82, 180
effectiveness, 54, 65, 120
Einstein, 130
element, 5, 17, 28, 61, 65, 72, 77, 82,
86, 93, 101, 116, 122, 128,
150, 176, 178
embrace, 4, 6, 17, 20, 23–25, 31, 33,
41, 45, 46, 52, 59, 64, 86,
93, 95, 98, 109, 115, 117,
128, 130, 134, 151, 160,
167, 170, 177, 178,
180–183
emergence, 10
Eminem, 40, 45
emotion, 40, 45, 89, 131
empathy, 117
emphasis, 16, 57, 81, 101, 175
employ, 143, 171
empowerment, 10, 13, 15
encouragement, 178
end, 86

Index

endeavor, 134, 179
energy, 54, 117, 122, 130, 181
engage, 7, 16, 28, 66, 83, 118, 121, 129, 130, 146, 181
engagement, 14, 27, 117, 119, 124, 134, 146, 167, 182, 183
enjoyment, 43
entertainment, 21, 92
enthusiasm, 181
environment, 4, 13, 97, 100, 113, 180, 181
equation, 2, 3, 6, 11, 12, 14, 23, 28, 42, 45, 60, 72, 75, 81, 94, 101, 110, 114, 117, 122, 124, 128, 130, 137, 140, 142, 144, 146, 167, 177–179
error, 109
essence, 37, 62, 129, 179
everyday, 2, 36
evolution, 10, 147, 181, 183
exaggeration, 93
example, 4, 11, 12, 17, 36, 39, 43, 49, 59, 64, 86–89, 92, 96, 101, 108, 112, 114, 116, 133, 144, 160, 162, 163, 170–172, 178, 182
exchange, 10, 125
excitement, 28, 57
exercise, 17, 48, 49, 68, 125, 149
exhalation, 126
expansion, 10
experience, 1, 20, 21, 55, 69, 71, 81, 83, 86, 91, 93, 96, 98, 111, 116, 119–121, 130, 137, 140, 144, 145, 158, 167, 177
experiment, 36, 44, 62, 86, 100, 108, 112

experimentation, 4, 20, 31, 69, 84, 103, 110, 179
exploration, 69, 147, 179, 180
explore, 6, 11, 15, 16, 40, 47, 49, 57, 59, 62, 64, 70, 72, 74, 84, 91, 95, 98, 103, 105, 108, 110, 134, 137, 146, 151, 158, 163, 164, 170, 183
exposure, 10
expression, 4, 11, 13, 14, 28, 31, 33, 45, 47, 52, 85, 90, 97, 100, 108, 110, 112, 117, 140, 144, 145, 151, 158, 176, 180, 183

fabric, 165, 170
face, 15, 105, 117, 133, 182
familiarity, 27
family, 179–181
fan, 170, 182
fear, 4, 137, 139
feature, 4, 74, 85, 87, 151
feedback, 179, 183
feel, 3, 16, 20, 40–42, 49, 55, 63, 82, 95, 109, 130, 135, 139, 152, 181, 182
feeling, 62, 64
fellow, 95, 100, 102, 174, 177–179
fight, 158
finding, 72, 95, 96, 100, 112
fire, 40, 171, 178
flair, 128, 163, 182
flavor, 2, 163
flaw, 85, 98, 115, 130, 151
flawlessness, 4
flight, 158
flow, 4, 5, 15, 19, 20, 23, 28, 31, 36, 38–40, 42–45, 47, 49, 52, 64, 67, 77, 81–86, 89, 92,

    93, 96, 106, 111–114, 119,
        124, 125, 128, 130, 133,
        140, 144, 158, 160,
        163–165, 171, 178
fluidity, 5
focus, 48, 156, 158, 169, 183
following, 4, 15–17, 20, 22, 24, 28,
        29, 36, 39, 41, 43, 44, 46,
        54, 58, 65, 66, 68, 70, 72,
        75, 77, 82, 83, 88, 89, 91,
        92, 97–99, 113–116, 118,
        122, 128–130, 137,
        139–141, 147–149, 152,
        156, 159, 182
force, 1, 11, 13, 15
form, 9, 21, 72, 101, 140, 145, 183
format, 173
formula, 96
foster, 95, 123, 134
foundation, 106
fourth, 68, 171
framework, 86, 115, 122, 165
freedom, 45
freestyle, 113
freestyling, 182
freewriting, 4
frequency, 23, 53, 75, 108, 113, 155, 157
friend, 179
fry, 96, 109
fun, 49, 82
function, 6, 27, 28, 53, 81, 117, 179
funk, 171
fusion, 10
future, 11, 102, 146, 149, 183

game, 47
generation, 151

genre, 3, 5, 9–13, 28, 35, 70, 71, 96,
        105, 129, 151, 164, 170,
        172–176, 181, 183
glimpse, 2
globalization, 10
go, 5, 25, 31, 34, 47, 59, 64, 140
goal, 3, 20, 47, 69, 74
gold, 91, 178
grid, 64
grime, 10
groove, 11, 16, 26, 38, 57, 62–64, 111
groundwork, 10, 13
growth, 144, 147, 177
guard, 24
guide, 6, 55, 59, 100, 109, 140, 177, 179
guitar, 70

hallmark, 114–116
hat, 60, 61, 63, 64
health, 157, 161
healthcare, 157, 163
heart, 6, 15, 151, 178
heartbeat, 21, 40, 83, 136
heartbreak, 89
help, 37, 45, 47–50, 53, 57, 60, 113,
        125, 131, 137–139,
        155–160, 162, 163
hesitation, 87, 112
hi, 60, 61, 63, 64
hic, 50, 53, 155
Hiccup, 94, 101, 110, 117
hiccup, 2, 3, 6, 23–25, 27, 28, 30, 39,
        41, 43, 53, 55, 58–64,
        72–77, 81–89, 91–93, 95,
        96, 98–121, 124, 126,
        128–131, 133, 134, 140,
        143–146, 149–152, 156,

Index

160–165, 167–169, 175–178, 182, 183
highlight, 124, 168, 176, 183
hindrance, 33
hip, 3–7, 9–11, 13–15, 28, 29, 31, 35–38, 40, 42, 45, 47, 49, 52, 55, 57, 59, 62, 64, 66, 68–71, 74, 81–83, 85, 88, 89, 91–93, 95–97, 100–108, 110, 112, 114, 115, 117, 120, 121, 123, 129, 131, 140, 142, 144–147, 149, 155, 158, 163–165, 174–176, 179–183
history, 11
hit, 45, 61, 82
homogenization, 10
hook, 20
hop, 3–7, 9–11, 13–15, 28, 29, 31, 35–38, 40, 42, 45, 47, 49, 52, 55, 57, 59, 62, 64, 66, 68–71, 74, 81–83, 85, 88, 89, 91–93, 95–97, 100–108, 110, 112, 114, 115, 117, 120, 121, 123, 129, 131, 140, 142, 144–147, 149, 155, 158, 163–165, 174–176, 179–183
hope, 163
humble, 9
humor, 46, 91–93, 106, 130, 145, 164, 182, 183
hydration, 156

idea, 3, 29, 33, 63, 65, 133, 140, 181
identity, 5, 9, 11, 13, 86, 101, 110, 134, 175, 176, 178

image, 133
imagery, 12
impact, 23, 40, 68, 82, 111, 122, 151, 155, 162, 163, 165, 180, 182
imperfection, 4, 33, 178, 183
implementation, 65
importance, 35, 100, 108, 160, 180
improvisation, 36, 127–129
impulse, 72
inclusion, 150
incongruity, 92
inconvenience, 28, 125
incorporate, 10, 16, 17, 26, 27, 30, 36, 44, 45, 49, 52, 58, 60, 62, 64, 66, 73, 77, 81, 101, 106, 108, 112, 114, 117, 119, 127, 130, 145, 165, 182, 183
incorporating, 7, 41, 52, 57, 68, 72, 76, 78, 82–86, 88, 90, 91, 105, 107, 108, 118, 127, 159, 163, 179
incorporation, 12, 28, 121, 149, 163, 175
increase, 183
individual, 101, 178
individuality, 3, 95, 97, 144, 149, 175
industry, 1, 10, 35, 143, 177
influence, 10, 11, 13, 25, 182
ingredient, 83
inhalation, 126
innovation, 4, 28, 33, 78, 100, 113, 151, 164, 176, 178
inspiration, 6, 17, 35–37, 69, 76, 100, 165, 169, 170, 178, 181
instance, 12, 16, 36, 40, 41, 45, 61, 64, 87, 89, 94, 98, 109,

111, 113, 119, 129, 130, 133, 145, 163, 171, 177–179, 182
intake, 50, 65
integral, 110, 117, 180
integrating, 38, 39, 50, 58, 122, 140, 168
integration, 31, 103, 144, 164
integrity, 10, 87
intensity, 82, 104, 108
interaction, 41, 119–121, 130, 133, 145, 180, 181
internet, 10
interplay, 40, 61, 83, 146, 178
interpretation, 182
interruption, 41, 49, 160
intersection, 164
intimacy, 104
irregularity, 26
irritation, 161
issue, 60, 87, 157

J. Cole, 167
jargon, 174–176
jazz, 10, 36
journal, 37
journey, 1, 2, 9, 11, 23, 25, 28, 45, 59, 66, 97, 102, 110, 114, 121, 142, 147–149, 158, 160, 170, 179, 180
joy, 121
justice, 15

Kendrick, 20, 82
Kendrick Lamar, 12, 40
Kendrick Lamar's, 40
key, 28, 31, 38, 42, 44, 62, 64, 86, 88, 93, 101, 112, 113, 122, 130, 146, 152, 158, 170, 174
kick, 59–61, 64
kind, 124
king, 103
knowledge, 177, 178

lack, 13, 45, 47
Lamar, 68
landscape, 2, 13, 88, 101, 110, 117, 140, 144, 165, 183
language, 4, 45, 174, 176
latter, 108, 183
laugh, 119, 130, 133, 182
laughter, 92, 117, 119, 136
layer, 41, 45, 57, 59, 60, 63, 82, 86, 100, 145, 182
layering, 6, 59–61
leaps, 67, 68
learning, 20, 144, 158
legacy, 13
lens, 3, 28, 94, 110, 163, 167, 175
level, 5, 16, 36, 47, 83, 93, 112, 124
lexicon, 170, 174–176
lie, 2
life, 2, 31, 36, 72, 75, 93, 133, 162
lifeblood, 181
light, 52
likelihood, 52, 125, 158
Lil Dicky, 182
Lil Wayne, 173
limitation, 100, 127
line, 12, 20, 39, 41, 43, 45, 82, 86, 89
listener, 15, 20, 38, 40, 43, 57, 59, 61, 68, 69, 81, 89, 112, 167
listening, 71, 83, 111, 116
live, 7, 12, 114, 119, 130, 137, 145
Lizzo, 133
love, 179, 181, 183

Index 195

lyric, 108, 114
lyricism, 4
lyricist, 1

magic, 99
mainstream, 2, 10
making, 4, 11, 12, 15, 17, 20, 28, 30, 64, 66, 72, 82, 83, 86, 89, 105, 109, 119, 121, 123, 130, 160, 172, 182, 183
management, 52, 163
managing, 7, 47, 49, 54, 55, 113, 139, 155, 161
manipulation, 74, 75
mark, 45
master, 57
masterpiece, 142
mastery, 20, 47, 81
material, 36
materialism, 10
means, 145–147, 164, 175
mechanism, 161
media, 10, 181, 182
melody, 67, 96
melting, 9
member, 179
mentor, 177
mentorship, 177
message, 10, 20, 45
metaphor, 93, 182
method, 64, 121, 126, 138, 156, 159
mind, 100, 159
mindset, 4, 45, 113, 114, 139
misstep, 3
mix, 60
modulation, 106
moment, 2, 38, 41, 55, 87, 89, 92, 112, 119, 129, 130, 133, 140, 144, 145, 147

mood, 133
move, 5, 15, 16, 179
movement, 9, 13, 15, 16, 52–55, 57
multiple, 50, 106, 163, 164
muscle, 53, 158, 159
music, 1, 3, 5–7, 10–13, 15, 16, 21, 23–28, 31, 35–37, 40, 44, 49, 57–59, 62, 64–66, 68, 69, 72, 73, 77, 81–85, 97, 98, 101, 103, 105, 107–111, 115–117, 133, 140, 143, 144, 147, 149, 152, 160, 163–165, 167, 170, 174, 177–179, 181–183
musician, 36, 158
myriad, 2

name, 1
narrative, 12, 23, 46, 89, 94, 111, 112, 116, 131, 133
Nas, 12
nature, 6, 23, 25, 48, 58, 59, 62, 64–66, 88, 91, 93, 110, 117, 130, 145, 146, 158, 164, 170, 173, 177, 183
necessity, 128
neck, 52
need, 45, 47, 112, 142
neighborhood, 9
nerve, 156, 162
nervousness, 137
network, 101
New York City, 9, 13
night, 179
nostalgia, 149
note, 41, 61, 98
nuisance, 17, 112, 161
number, 38

occurrence, 47, 49, 155, 157, 158
off, 4, 24, 58, 61, 64, 133
one, 2, 38, 96, 102, 124, 139, 155, 168, 178
opportunity, 23, 55, 112, 130, 144, 160
originality, 115
other, 3, 6, 95–98, 100, 101, 162, 178
outlet, 9, 54
output, 6, 101, 179
oxygen, 125

pacing, 86
paralysis, 4, 33
paranoia, 68
part, 86, 102, 110, 114, 117, 121–123, 134, 142, 149, 177, 180, 182
participate, 181
participation, 131, 145
passion, 179, 181
patient, 162
pattern, 26, 38, 41, 59, 62–64, 86, 87, 126, 163
pause, 39, 43, 81, 86, 96, 108, 119, 130, 145, 177
pay, 43, 170
people, 9, 11, 15, 16, 94
percussion, 6, 59, 60, 62, 63
perfection, 3–5, 47, 143
perfectionism, 4, 25, 34
performance, 7, 23, 47, 49, 50, 52, 55, 81–83, 112–114, 117, 119, 121, 122, 125, 127–131, 133, 135–137, 140, 144–146, 158, 160, 177
performer, 1, 123, 134, 145

period, 157, 162
person, 95
persona, 121–124, 180
personality, 110
perspective, 3, 66, 113, 180
Pharrell Williams, 172
phase, 60
phenomenon, 3, 11, 15, 65, 83
phrasing, 42, 43, 84
piece, 38
pitch, 64–66, 75
place, 23, 61, 69, 86
placement, 59, 89, 164
play, 40, 64, 86, 88, 104, 145, 156, 158, 181
playing, 41
playlist, 168, 169
point, 119
pollination, 10
polyrhythm, 11
pose, 71, 128
positivity, 133
posture, 47
pot, 9
potential, 7, 26, 28, 35, 52, 55, 62, 66, 67, 69, 71, 73, 87, 114, 117, 121, 122, 128, 151, 157, 161
poverty, 9, 13
power, 11, 23, 34, 55, 104, 141, 149, 152, 173, 181
practice, 20, 37, 49, 68, 84, 85, 93, 114, 127, 140, 158, 169, 177
precision, 45
predictability, 82
preparation, 52, 131, 139, 140
presence, 7, 122, 125, 140
pressure, 33, 94, 137

Index

principle, 2
procedure, 162
process, 6, 45, 47, 52, 64, 65, 67, 74, 99, 103, 108, 109, 112, 116, 133, 141, 147, 159, 170, 177, 179–183
producer, 1, 171
product, 14
production, 3, 10, 25, 27, 72, 74, 99, 100, 161, 170, 179
professional, 157
progress, 7
proliferation, 182
prone, 49, 100–102, 137, 143, 144, 178
prowess, 5
pulse, 1, 62, 83
punctuation, 101
pursuit, 5, 87

quality, 10, 30, 60, 61, 70, 109, 125, 162
quest, 163
quirk, 149, 167
quirkiness, 164
quo, 9

racism, 9
radio, 2
range, 170, 174
rap, 20, 145, 182
rapper, 3, 41, 177, 178, 180
rawness, 3
reach, 147, 152
reaction, 176
realization, 179
realm, 64, 66, 69, 83, 91, 147
record, 171
recording, 72, 74

reduction, 60
reflection, 45, 147, 149
reflex, 76, 126, 156, 161, 162
reggae, 10
reign, 91, 129, 158
relatability, 6, 91, 94, 95, 122–124, 142, 145
relationship, 52, 75, 123, 134, 137, 140, 181
relaxation, 47, 48, 50, 52, 53, 157–160
release, 52, 54, 61, 84, 159
relief, 162, 163
remedy, 52
reminder, 95, 131, 181
repetition, 30
representation, 42, 75, 145
research, 163
resilience, 1, 10–12, 148
resonance, 12, 83, 94
resource, 170
resourcefulness, 168
response, 9, 12, 61, 117, 126, 137, 158
result, 94
rhyme, 3, 6, 45, 85–88, 171
rhythm, 3, 16, 17, 20, 23, 24, 28, 38, 40–42, 49, 52, 55, 57, 59, 61, 62, 64, 77, 81, 83–86, 103, 105, 106, 108, 110, 113, 114, 125, 131, 136, 140, 144, 145, 158, 163–165, 170
richness, 181
right, 62, 89, 112, 158
rigidity, 82
rise, 10, 182
risk, 113, 137
rock, 70

role, 10, 12, 53, 64, 156, 158, 177, 179, 181
room, 130
routine, 49, 52, 53, 127, 158–160

sample, 61, 74, 75, 171
sampling, 6, 27, 72–74
scenario, 61, 92, 113
scene, 182
scheme, 86–88, 171
second, 64, 86, 171
section, 11, 13, 16, 21, 23, 25, 28, 35, 40, 47, 49, 52, 57, 59, 62, 64, 67, 69, 72, 74, 76, 81, 86, 91, 95, 98, 100, 103, 105, 108, 110, 112, 115, 117, 121, 125, 127, 130, 134, 137, 140, 149, 155, 158, 161, 163, 165, 168, 170, 174, 179, 181
selection, 165, 168
self, 2, 4, 33, 45, 110, 133, 182
sense, 3, 9, 13, 16, 28, 41, 57, 68, 84, 95, 104, 123, 133, 159, 181
series, 147
set, 17, 64, 95, 109
setting, 35
share, 7, 10, 95, 102, 152, 178, 179, 181, 182
sharing, 95, 131, 152
shift, 10, 64, 113, 114, 139
shoulder, 52
show, 121
showcase, 140, 169, 182
signature, 93, 95, 101, 108–110, 116, 122, 150
significance, 11, 176, 181
sing, 70
sister, 179

size, 124
skill, 23, 140
slang, 174–176
sleep, 19
smile, 130
snare, 59–61, 64
socio, 9, 12, 13
software, 10
solidarity, 9, 178
song, 5, 21, 24, 42, 68, 71, 111, 163, 164, 172
songwriting, 23, 25
sound, 4, 5, 7, 10, 23, 25, 28, 41, 44, 50, 53, 59, 60, 65, 66, 69–72, 74, 83, 85, 88, 95, 97–101, 105, 106, 108–110, 115, 117, 131, 142, 149–151, 155, 160, 163, 165
soundscape, 149
source, 17, 33, 78, 100, 102, 178
space, 81, 83, 95, 100, 179
spark, 129
speech, 133, 140
spirit, 1, 15, 88
spontaneity, 25, 82, 106, 117, 128, 129, 140, 146, 182
stability, 47
stage, 15, 119, 121–125, 129, 137–140, 159, 177, 180
standard, 33
standpoint, 28
state, 52, 158, 160
status, 9, 11
step, 2, 73, 108, 115, 128
story, 9, 21–23, 89, 93, 121, 131, 133, 144, 177
storytelling, 2, 5, 6, 12, 21, 22, 28, 46, 81, 83, 84, 91, 168, 169

Index

strategy, 112
strength, 102
stress, 48, 50, 53, 94, 137, 158, 160
stretching, 52
structure, 23, 28, 38, 89, 130
struggle, 4, 10, 12, 27, 47, 82, 84, 93, 112
studio, 99
stutter, 3, 96
style, 4, 12, 44, 57, 62, 88, 93, 108–110, 114, 116, 117, 121, 122, 167, 177
sub, 10
subsection, 9
success, 10
succession, 108
sufferer, 177
sum, 101
summary, 165
support, 100, 102, 178–181
supreme, 33, 91, 121, 129, 158
surprise, 16, 24, 27, 28, 38, 40, 57, 62, 69, 82, 112, 117, 128
swing, 16
symbol, 151
symptom, 157
syncopation, 6, 16, 26, 28, 40, 57, 59, 61, 62, 64, 68, 77
synergy, 95–98, 100, 101, 169
system, 48, 113, 137, 161

t, 3, 85
table, 2, 181
take, 2, 26, 49, 55, 74, 124, 147, 149, 182
tapestry, 23, 41, 59, 93, 95, 149, 167, 181
teacher, 177

technique, 12, 41, 48, 59, 61, 62, 74, 83, 101, 111–114, 125, 126, 130, 137, 159
technology, 10
temperature, 50
tempo, 16, 24
tensing, 159
tension, 38, 43, 52, 61, 62, 84, 106, 158, 159
test, 148
testament, 11, 88, 149, 151, 168, 182
texture, 58, 60, 77, 88, 96, 98, 105, 112, 140
theme, 87, 95
theory, 3, 16, 28, 57, 59, 62, 64, 66, 67, 69, 74, 81, 84, 92, 103, 105, 117, 120, 127, 163, 169
third, 171
thoracic, 53
thought, 35, 45, 168
Timbaland, 172
time, 9, 16, 23, 55, 69, 75, 83, 129, 140, 145, 149, 180
timing, 42, 43, 64, 84, 88, 93, 122, 145, 164
today, 9, 10
tool, 6, 26, 28, 54, 59, 76, 81, 91, 95, 100, 117, 122, 175, 176
total, 60, 172
track, 16, 17, 33, 43, 60, 61, 70, 74, 82, 98, 105, 106, 111, 112, 114, 150, 171, 178, 182
transformation, 11
transition, 160
trap, 10
treatment, 163
trial, 109

trigger, 158
trill, 49
triplet, 41
triumph, 93
trust, 135
turn, 2, 52, 92, 102, 124, 127, 128, 140, 144
turning, 7, 40, 98, 122, 130, 133, 151, 176, 178

unconventionality, 35
understanding, 20, 28, 31, 38, 55, 59, 62, 64, 66, 69, 74, 95, 100, 106, 122, 144, 160, 163, 165, 170, 174, 179, 180
unemployment, 13
unexpectedness, 93
uniqueness, 44, 95, 102, 167
unpredictability, 17, 23, 24, 28, 44, 64, 69, 87, 112, 114, 117, 122, 130, 140, 163, 177
up, 28, 49, 52, 54, 74, 159
urgency, 40, 68, 167
use, 4, 12, 16, 29, 42, 43, 45, 59, 61, 66–71, 74, 81, 83, 88, 105, 109, 111, 112, 130, 139, 145, 146, 163, 164, 168, 175

variation, 61
variety, 73, 75, 88, 161, 163
versatility, 2, 164
verse, 41, 49, 86, 119, 130, 133, 145, 171
view, 94
violence, 9, 10
vision, 1, 110, 179–181

visualization, 140, 160
vocal, 3, 7, 11, 13, 28, 49, 50, 52, 53, 57, 65, 68, 95–98, 101, 103, 105–110, 134, 139, 155, 158, 160, 168, 169, 182
vocalist, 98
voice, 9, 13, 14, 20, 21, 23, 27, 47, 95, 98, 102, 108, 149, 178
vulnerability, 7, 36, 46, 89, 93, 104, 123, 131, 135, 142, 144–146

walk, 179
warm, 49, 50, 52, 139
waveform, 72
way, 11, 26, 31, 44, 64, 81, 85, 102, 113, 129, 130, 146, 149
weapon, 121
weight, 36, 40, 82, 89
well, 83, 158, 160, 172
willingness, 20, 31, 69, 100, 146
word, 20, 40, 45
wordplay, 93
work, 2, 4, 5, 11, 12, 40, 64, 165, 180–183
world, 1–3, 10, 21, 23, 25, 28, 33, 35, 40, 47, 72, 74, 76, 81, 85, 95, 100, 103, 105, 108, 112, 114, 117, 121, 129, 140, 144, 149, 158, 163, 165, 167, 170, 174, 176, 181
writing, 4, 35, 36, 45, 47, 49, 52, 55, 147, 179, 181

yourself, 17, 23, 135, 139, 160